COUNTRY RISK: A THEORETICAL FRAMEWORK OF ANALYSIS

ABOUT THE AUTHOR

Anna Micaela Ciarrapico has done research at LUISS University, Rome. She was awarded a Master degree in Economics by the London School of Economics and Political Sciences (U.K.). At present, she is a research fellow in economics at the University of Molise, Campobasso and a lecturer in Theory and Practice of Planning Methods at the LUISS.

She has published various works on labour economics, inequality economics and country risk.

COUNTRY RISK: A THEORETICAL FRAMEWORK OF ANALYSIS

Anna Micaela Ciarrapico

Dartmouth

Aldershot · Brookfield USA · Hong Kong · Singapore · Sydney

Published by
Dartmouth Publishing Company Limited
Gower House
Croft Road
Aldershot
Hants GU11 3HR
England

Dartmouth Publishing Company Limited
Distributed in the United States by
Ashgate Publishing Group
Old Post Road
Brookfield
Vermont 05036
USA

A CIP catalogue record for this book is available from
the British Library and the US Library of Congress

Reprinted 1997

ISBN 1 85521 099 1

Printed and bound in Great Britain by Intype, London

Laserset by Computype Manuscript Services, Standard House, 49 Lawrence Street, York

Contents

List of tables

List of figures

Introduction

"In the early 1970s the total debt of developing countries was less than a 100 billion dollars. By the end of the eighties it has passed the trillion dollar mark. In the meantime, however, everybody lost the illusion that the debt would be repaid in full."

These few words written by Daniel Cohen (1989) give a very clear idea of the actual state of the developing country foreign debt situation. But what has happened in the last two decades?

In the 70s lenders appeared not to be concerned with the risk associated with international lending. In part this was because the economic situation was one of high export growth and low interest rates. When interest rates are below export growth rates, exports grow faster than debt and borrowers can borrow the amount needed to service their debt without experiencing a rise in the debt-to-export ratio.

Moreover banks were apparently not concerned with the question of whether the borrowing countries would be willing or able to pay back their debts, or even service them, out of their own resources. With interest rates below the growth rates of the debtor's economies, new lending to repay old loans made sense.

Borrowing countries were never scrutinized as to whether the loans were being put to good use and whether the economic policies were sound. But the favourable state of nature of high export growth and low interest rates could not last forever.

Looking at the past, however, it seems as if lenders, and also borrowers in some respects, did not take into account the possibility of a switch in the relationship between growth and interest rates.

Anyway the switch took place, abruptly, at the beginning of the 80s. Tight monetary policies implemented in industrialized countries to slow down the rise in prices caused a sudden and sharp rise in real interest rates, a fall in export prices and terms of trade of developing countries and consequently a collapse in their export earnings.

Banks, however, did not stop or slow their cross-border lending activity. In two years, 1980–1981, total bank exposure nearly doubled above the level of 1979 in the major countries. Banks, on the other hand, abruptly withdrew new credits starting in 1982. New market-based lending to developing countries virtually disappeared after 1982. Even when lending continued, the borrowing countries paid more to the commercial banks than they received in new funds.

In August 1982 Mexico announced that it was unable to service its external debt of approximately 80 billion dollars. This was the onset of the crisis.

Banks began to be concerned about the borrowing countries willingness or ability to repay their loans.

In the summer of 1982 lenders understood, at their cost, the unsecured nature of sovereign debts, the primary example being the fact that Mexico's oil wealth could not be considered collateral at all. In the case of Mexico, the repayment of loans depended upon the Mexican government's willingness to impose on the population the austerity measures which were required to transfer to lender countries whatever income was needed to service the debt.

From the theoretical point of view the uncollateralized nature of sovereign debt started to be analyzed and with it the specific nature of debt rescheduling agreements, the risk of a bank panic, the inefficiency of the credit market when lenders lack the capability of committing themselves to a lending policy and all other features of the credit market to sovereign nations which are direct consequences of the absence of a collateral.

From the borrower's point of view the question which arose in 1982 concerned the evaluation by the debtors of costs and benefits associated to the service of the debt. Would the penalties that the lender could impose on a borrowing country be sufficient to induce borrowing countries not to default?

So the focus of country risk analysis moved from the prediction of the credit worthiness of countries through the use of statistical methods to the analysis of features and determinants of the supply and demand of sovereign loans.

Country risk analysis in the 70s sought to identify those cases where borrowing countries would be unable to meet their commitments on external debt. The most sophisticated models used logit and discriminant analyses to estimate the probability of default defined as a function of a certain number of explanatory variables. These models gave evidence of many statistical problems such as the use of reschedulings as a proxy for outright defaults and the existence of multicollinearity between the independent variables. But, apart from these difficulties, the models lacked a rigourous theoretical framework in which the special features and determinants of the supply and demand of foreign loans could be studied so that some light could be shed on the circumstances under which debt problems might arise. So, the evolution of the theory of country risk on one side and the many important questions raised by the new economic setting and by the developing countries debt situation, on the other hand, ask for a more complete framework of analysis.

What the subsequent chapters seek to provide is a detailed picture of how country risk analysis evolved over time going from the "practical" methods of country risk assessment developed by banks towards a "pure theory of country risk" as the one presented in the most sophisticated papers written by well known economists. The main aim of the book is that of giving a general, theoretical framework of analysis in which the determinants of the demand and supply of foreign loan may be identified specifying many, special features which characterize the cross-border lending activity of commercial banks and the nature of borrowers.

WHAT IS COUNTRY RISK AND HOW IT MATERIALISES

To banks international debt is a possible way of investing their capital but it also means the possibility of exposure to a loss. Money definitions have been given of country risk but we want to refer to those which, according to us, are the more appropriate, straightforward and useful ones.

A general definition given by Nagy (1979) states that country risk is the exposure to a loss in cross-border lending caused by events which are, at least to some extent, under the control of the government of the borrowing country.

Therefore country risk only concerns cross-border loans; all lending in a country is exposed to country risk; only events which are at least to some extent under the control of government can lead to the materialisation of country risk.

Country risk, as defined above, is a broader concept than sovereign risk which is the risk of lending directly to the government of a sovereign nation.

Moreover according to the above definition, country risk as opposed to commercial risk is defined as exposure to a loss due to events which are under the control of a private enterprise or individual but not under the control of the government.

The distinction between country risk and commercial risk focusses on whether or not the cause of the materialisation of risk is under the control of the government of the borrowing country.

A different definition (Heffernan (1986)) does not distinguish between country risk and sovereign risk and defines country (or sovereign) risk as the risk associated with publicly guaranteed loans or loans made directly to a foreign government.

According to this definition, country risk is opposed to private risk, the risk associated with non publicly guaranteed private external loans. The distinction here is conceptually based on whom rests the ultimate responsibility for repayment.

In the following chapters when we speak of country risk we refer to the second definition we gave: that is, country risk is the risk associated with publicly guaranteed loans or with loans made directly to foreign governments.

It is however important to stress that banks do not usually distinguish private commercial risk from general sovereign (or country) risk. This is so because lenders can often act so as to force the government to intervene and to make good on a loan. A good example is the one reported by Diaz-Alejandro (1985) regarding commercial non-guaranteed loans to private Chilean banks. Having invested the money borrowed recklessly, the private Chilean banks failed to repay their debts. The foreign lender banks threatened to worsen the Chilean government's own credit terms if it did not assume these debts. The Chilean government at the end decided to do so!

Country risk materialises when a country is unable to meet its commitments on external debt.

The materialisation of country risk, however, can take different forms. The debtor may notify the creditor that he will not make any further service payments because he can not or does not want to pay *(default)* or because he does not recognise the debt *(repudiation)*. The bank loss is consequently equal to the part of the principal not repaid plus the interests forgone.

Alternatively the debtor can *renegotiate* the debt. The creditor, in this case, receives less from the debtor than originally agreed because, for example, the interest rate is lowered or the spread narrowed, or because part of the principal will not be repaid.

The debtor may also decide *to reschedule* or to *ask for a moratorium.* Rescheduling and moratorium both imply the lengthening of the terms of the loan.

When a country reschedules, the terms of the loan are lengthened because annual repayments of the principal are of a smaller amount and spread over a greater number of years than originally agreed.

When we have a moratorium, the terms of the loan are lengthened because there will be a grace period for the repayment of principal. In both cases (rescheduling and moratorium) the interest rate remains the same. The only measurable loss for the lender is the cost of negotiating the rescheduling or the moratorium.

Country risk can also materialise as *technical default*. The borrower temporarily fails to meet the terms for debt-service payments because of his inability or unwillingness to pay or because of administrative delays or inefficiencies.

1 Different approaches to country risk assessment

We first want to analyze that part of the literature on country risk consisting of methods aimed at predicting the credit worthiness of borrowing countries.

All these methods were developed essentially in the early and mid seventies when the cross-border lending activity of commercial banks was very intense.

The possibility of a default on foreign debt was feared by commercial banks which tried to develop statistical methods of country risk assessment also able to predict in advance debt problems arising.

The assessment of country risk is the evaluation of whether debt-servicing problems will arise or not.

There are informal methods for assessing country risk, consisting of economic and political descriptive information and indicators regarding the borrowing country. With the help of such information and indicators the analyst formulates judgments about how "risky" a country is, judgments which may be expressed in a systemic form (i.e. rating) or in a descriptive form (i.e. good risk, poor risk).

There are also formal systems of assessment, such as checklists and statistical systems, whose structure is rigid and well defined. In the literature on country risk four types of system are commonly distinguished: i) fully qualitative; ii) structural qualitative; iii) checklist and iv) other quantitative.

This classification first appeared in Stephen Goodman's article "How the big US banks really evaluate sovereign risk" and derived from an Eximbank survey of 37 US banks' sovereign risk evaluation procedures. Goodman remarked that the analytical evaluation approaches taken ranged from the strictly qualitative, involving no numerical or statistical analysis, to the fundamentally quantitative in character.

Fully qualitative systems basically consist of a country evaluation report of no fixed format, the analytical content varying from country to country. The absence of a definite framework of analysis to apply to all countries makes it impossible to undertake cross-country comparisons. Moreover, these evaluation systems inevitably tend to be retrospective rather than prospective.

Structured qualitative systems generate country reports according to a standardized format, with well defined scope and some kind of statistical analysis generally included. Because of the standardized format, cross-country comparisons are possible.

The checklist system is quantitative in character. It consists of a set of economic, financial, social and political indicators that are compiled for all the borrowing countries the bank is interested in. It is useful to distinguish between weighted and unweighted checklists.

In the former, each variable is subjectively weighted according to the analyst's preferred emphasis on relevant factors. In the latter all variables are given the same weight. The variables chosen are quantitative or quantifiable and can thus be aggregated into a summary rating for each country. This method is often criticized as "subjective" because of the subjective judgement implicit in the selection and the weighting of the variables.

"Other quantitative" systems, finally, include econometric and other statistical methodologies for the assessment of country risk. It is believed that these techniques offer the most objective, systematic and comparative way to assess a country's credit creditworthiness.

1.1 FULLY QUALITATIVE SYSTEMS

Not much more needs to be said about the fully qualitative systems. As noted, they consist of a report that is a general discussion of a country's economic, political and social conditions and prospects. The use of such systems constitutes an intermediate stage in the country evaluation project, as banks seek to develop a more highly structured system suitable to their needs.

1.2 STRUCTURED QUALITATIVE SYSTEMS

Structured qualitative systems, as noted, have a standard format and include some statistics. Usually the country evaluation report focuses on economic and political factors. The economic situation of the prospective borrowing country is examined with an analysis of background factors, current internal indicators, current external indicators and the long-term and short-term aspects of creditworthiness.

As to political risk, the information generally considered includes the type of government, the orderliness of political succession, the homogeneity of the population, the quality of relationships with major trading partners and long-run social and political trends.

Usually the analyst writing the country report utilizes the data provided by what is called the "country spread sheet", a table where all the information given by different indicators is aggregated. As Hefferman (1986) reports, the components of the country spread sheet vary but in general there are six sections:

Section A =	Internal economic indicators
Section B =	Balance of payments
Section C =	Foreign Assets
Section D =	Debt structure
Section E =	Gross new debt
Section F =	Debt indicators

Internal economic indicators should give information on domestic economic policy. They usually include indicators of the size of economy (population, population growth, GDP, GDP *per capita*); growth indicators (GDP growth, unemployment rate) and inflation indicators such as consumer price index, money supply growth and budget deficit as a percentage of GDP.

According to some country risk analysts another relevant indicator is the share of investment in national income. A declining share presumably means that foreign capital is not being used only for investment purposes.

The second section of the spread sheet gives detailed data on the balance of payments (trade balance, current balance, capital account and their components, change in reserves).

External indicators should also provide an idea of how vulnerable a borrowing country's economy is to slowdowns in the world economy. To this purpose it is important to include a measure of the openness of the economy and to provide disaggregated data on imports and exports. The inclusion of information on the exchange rate is also useful.

The last four sections seek to give an idea of how creditworthy a country is.

Section C ordinarily reports data on international reserves, unutilised IMF credit and other foreign assets. Section D presents data on external debt (public and private, with their respective maturity structures). Section E gives information about gross new debt (public and private). And last, section F presents various debt indicators including the debt service ratio, debt as a percentage of GDP, the debt export ratio, foreign assets as a percentage of external debt.

Significant indicators of creditworthiness to be included in the spread sheet would be: the growth rate in external public or publicly guaranteed disbursed debt outstanding; variables that make it possible to assess the ability of the country to service its external debt; and an indicator of world liquidity, which could give an indication of the supply side of the foreign capital market.

1.3 CHECKLIST SYSTEMS

Essentially, the checklist resembles the country spread sheet just described. It is simply a list of statistics or questions which need to be answered to assess a borrowing country's creditworthiness. Checklist systems can be used either as an annex to the country report (then the checklist and the country spread sheet coincide) or as the functional equivalent thereof.

In the latter case each country is rated with respect to the various indicators or to general questions whose answers need personal judgment or first-hand knowledge of the country.

The score for each indicator is aggregated into a summary rating for the country. By the weighted checklist approach, each single score is assigned a subjectively determined weight; in the unweighted checklist all variables are weighted equally in determining the final score.

The variables included in the checklists are more or less the same as those that appear in the typical country spread sheet. The checklist may also include social and political variables such as indicators of political stability. Table 1.1 presents the variables that, according to the Eximbank survey, are usually included in checklist systems (S. Goodman 1978).

Table 1.1
Indicators included in checklist systems

Variable
I—Domestic economy
GNP
GNP per capita
Growth in GNP per capita
Inflation rate
Money supply growth
Investment-to-income ratio
Net budget position
Income growth fixed capital formation ratio
II—External economic variables
Exports and export growth
Imports and import growth
International reserves
Reserves import ratio
Trade and current account balances
Debt service ratio
IMF borrowings
Current collection experience of US suppliers
Debt service payments
Principal payments total external debt ratio
Share of gold in reserves
Share of leading non-oil export in total export revenue
Share of trade in GDP
Share of short-term credit in total credit
Total external debt
III—Social and political variables
Political stability
International banking division's region rating
Past trend in unemployment

1.4 OTHER QUANTITATIVE METHODS

When we speak of "other quantitative" methods for the assessment of country risk we refer to methods for gauging a country's debt servicing capacity that use relatively sophisticated statistical techniques. The "other quantitative" methods estimate the probability of a country's experiencing debt servicing difficulties as a function of a set of independent or explanatory variables.

The main problems a researcher is faced with are the choice of the dependent variable, the identification of economic variables able to explain why debt problems arise, and the choice of the most appropriate statistical technique.

1.4.1 Statistical techniques

The statistical procedures most frequently used for the assessment of country risk are discriminant analysis, logit analysis and principal component analysis.

Discriminant analysis

A classification problem, or discrimination problem, is one in which an object of given characteristics is to be classified into one of several alternative populations. In the case of country risk analysis, we want to know if a borrowing country belongs to the rescheduling group or to the non-rescheduling group.

Figure 1.1

The classification of borrowing countries

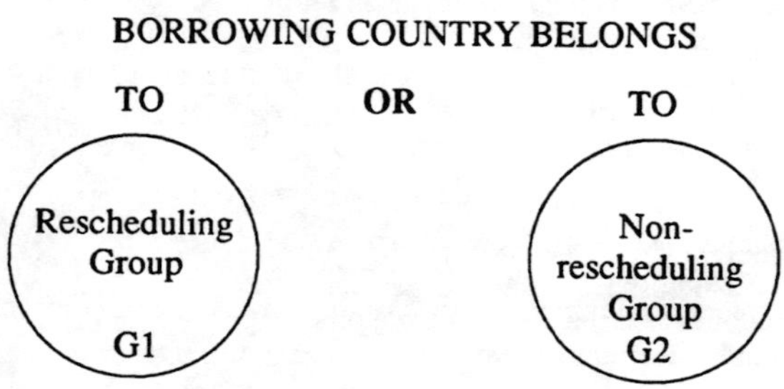

To make possible the classification of borrowing countries into one of the two relevant population groups, the first thing the analyst has to do is to select a sufficiently large sample of countries belonging to each of the two groups.

The binary classification is then obtained by the use of a discriminant function. This function is constructed as a linear combination of n explanatory variables. Hence we can write

$$Z = f(x_i) \qquad i = 1, 2, \ldots, n \tag{1}$$

or, more explicitly,

$$Z = \sum_{i=1}^{n} w_i x_i \qquad i = 1, 2, \ldots, n \tag{2}$$

where Z is the discriminant function, x_i the vector of the n independent variables and w_i the weights, or coefficients, attached to the explanatory variables. To choose the explanatory variables to insert in the discriminant function, first a general function is estimated.

In the estimation of the general function, the dependent variable is debt rescheduling and the independent variables are those believed to be relevant in explaining why debt problems arise. The variables which prove to be statistically significant and have the right sign are those that will appear in the discriminant function.

By the evaluation of the discriminant function, the Z-value for each of the borrowing countries under study may be computed. The computation of the Z-value for each rescheduling and non-rescheduling country allows us to obtain a frequency distribution of Z-values for each group. The determination of a critical Z-value, Z^*, is now required if the classification procedure is to go ahead. The critical Z-value is, in fact, used to differentiate: a country is classified as belonging to group G_1 if $Z < Z^*$; a country is classified as belonging to G_2 if $Z > Z^*$.

To maximize the linear discriminant function's ability to differentiate between members of the two groups, the weights, w_i, are assigned in such a way that the ratio of the variance between the two groups to the variance within the two groups is maximised.

However, the classification process is vulnerable to two different types of errors which we shall designate as Type I and Type II.

A Type I error is one where a country predicted not to reschedule does reschedule or better where a country belonging to G_1 is classified in G_2. A Type II error, conversely, is made when a country is predicted to reschedule but does not, that is the discriminant function assigns it to G_1 when it should belong to G_2.

An expected cost function is then formulated attaching costs and probabilities to these two types of error.

The discriminant function and the critical value for Z, Z^*, are determined jointly through an iterative procedure of minimisation of expected cost.

Logit analysis

Logit analysis is a dichotomous statistical analysis which deals with binary events. Applying logit analysis to country risk assessment means designating the binary event whether or not a country reschedules.

In logit models the probability of rescheduling is related to several economic variables.

We can write

$$y_i = \sum_{\substack{i=1 \\ j=1}}^{\substack{m \\ n}} b_j x_{ij} \tag{3}$$

Where y_i is the variable indicating the presence of a rescheduling and its value is unity for a rescheduling and zero otherwise; m is the number of explanatory variables, n the number of observations. In a logit model first an equation of this form is statistically estimated, possibly using maximum likelihood techniques.[1] Then, the resulting dependent variable, y, may be transformed into an indicator of the probability of rescheduling in the following way:

$$P_R = P_R(y_i = 1) = \frac{1}{(1 + e^{-y})} \tag{4}$$

In equation (4) P_R represents the indicator of the rescheduling probability and e is the base of the natural logarithm.

The value of the probability indicator can range from zero to one. Higher values of the predicted y indicate a higher probability of rescheduling, conditional on the country's values for explanatory variables. More precisely, the probability indicator equals one as the predicted y approaches infinity.

Again, it is necessary to choose a threshold probability, P_R^*, above which the prediction is of no rescheduling.[2]

Unlike the discriminant models where the critical Z^* value is determined jointly with the discriminant function, the choice of P_R^* is to some extent arbitrary.

Usually P_R^* is chosen in such a way as to minimize the total number of errors. Again a Type I error is made when a country not predicted to reschedule does, a Type II error when a country predicted to reschedule does not.

Figure 1.2

The relationship between the probability of rescheduling and the predicted $\bar{y}$

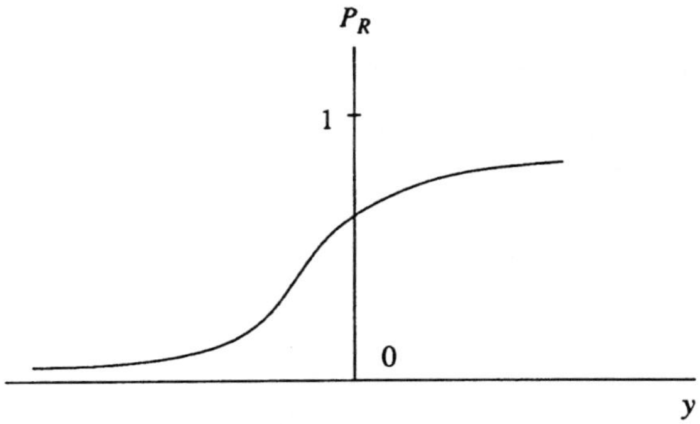

Principal components analysis

Even though principal components analysis has only been used once in country risk analysis (Dhonte 1974), it is worth explaining briefly the main characteristics of this statistical procedure. A set of components (or composite indicators) is substituted for the original group of indicators, and each component is a linear combination of all the original indicators.

A component, defined as

$$C_i = b_1x_1 + b_2x_2 + \ldots b_nx_n \tag{5}$$

is computed assuming that the sum of the n coefficients equals unity, and in such a way that the variance of equation (5) is maximized and the C_i, for all i, are orthogonal.

The relative importance of each component is measured by the proportion of total sample information it contains. We first compute the informational content of each component. This is equal to the sum of squares of distances of plots along that component. Expressing this sum as a percentage of the sample variance gives us the measure of the component's relative importance.

The principal components technique, then, consists of minimizing the sum of squares of the distance between the original plot and the components.

1.4.2 The choice of the dependent variable

The dependent variable employed by most statistical studies is the rescheduling of external debt, used as a proxy for default on sovereign loans. The choice of this variable can be ascribed to the fact that outright default and consequently debt repudiation by the borrower is very rare; hence the number of cases recorded do not constitute a large enough sample.

The rescheduling of a loan is an agreement between the borrowing country and the lending country to extend the maturity of the existing sovereign external debt. This agreement may sometimes represent a "good" event for the lender since a net present value gain may be recorded. Outright default, on the other hand, is always a bad event for lenders.

So if the purpose of a model is the estimation of the probability of default, the probability of rescheduling would appear to be a fairly weak proxy. The probability of rescheduling is a fine dependent variable, however, if the statistical models under analysis are seen as early warning models to signal the possibility of a rescheduling agreement because of the borrowing country's bad economic performance.

1.4.3 Significant explanatory variables

The choice of explanatory variables varies from model to model. We can nevertheless identify three main groups of causal variables: variables indicating the debt burden or the external debt position; foreign trade variables often indicating the liquidity position; and domestic economic variables or indicators.

In what follows, however, we only describe the variables used in the statistical models presented in Tables 1.2–1.12 and which seem to have some predictive ability in forecasting the probability of a country's having debt servicing problems.

The best known and most widely used indicator of debt servicing capacity is the debt service ratio (amortisation + interest payments/ earnings from exports of goods and services). This indicator measures the proportion of a country's foreign exchange earnings on current account that must be earmarked for debt servicing. Simple common sense suggests that there should be a positive correlation between this indicator and the danger of debt servicing problems: the higher this ratio, the more likely that the country will have to reschedule. A higher ratio, in fact, means a decline in foreign exchange earnings relative to the debt service burden or an increase in the debt service burden for a given level of reserves.

Another related indicator is the ratio of external debt outstanding to earnings from exports of goods and services. Compared to the debt service ratio, this indicator has a longer-term validity. Again, the correlation with the probability of rescheduling is positive.

A measure of the level of indebtedness is represented by the ratio of debt outstanding (or external debt) *to* gross national (or domestic) product. This indicator shows the size of the debt in relation to the economy's total resources. The higher the ratio, the greater the proportion of current output which will need to be diverted to debt servicing and the higher the probability of rescheduling.

Frank and Cline (1971) and Feder and Just (1977) propose as an explanatory variable for debt rescheduling the ratio of debt amortisation to total debt outstanding. This indicator is intended to pinpoint potential difficulties connected with the bunching of maturities, but it has provoked enormous controversy.

According to Frank and Cline, other things being equal, a low value of this indicator will be associated with a high probability of rescheduling. They argue that a country with a low amortisation ratio, indicating predominantly long-term debt liabilities, will have little short-term margin for reducing its debt service commitments by temporary reduction of borrowing, and moreover that difficult access to short-term commercial credit facilities indicates a "low degree" of creditworthiness.

Feder and Just included this variable in one of their models but excluded it from the other because of doubts about the causal relation between the probability of default or rescheduling and the average debt maturity (represented by the inverse of the amortisation/debt indicator). They stress that "it may well be that the loan maturity allowed by the lender depends on the country's debt servicing capacity; hence, the amortisation/debt ratio may be highly correlated with default without actually explaining any causal relationship".

Cline (1984) gives a different interpretation to this ratio. He claims that it represents the rate of amortisation and that, for a given debt-service ratio, a country with a higher amortisation rate will appear to have a stronger balance sheet to a lender and hence a smaller probability of rescheduling.

In the model proposed by Abassi and Taffler (1984), a variable that proves to be important and significant is loan commitment *per capita* (the ratio of new debt contracted during a given year to population). This variable, positively correlated with *per capita* GDP and external debt, is used as a proxy for wealth. The assumption is that countries showing high *per capita* loan commitments can borrow more because they are considered richer. And wealthier countries are less likely to reschedule.

Dhonte (1975) introduces two peculiar indicators: the ratio of debt service payments to disbursements and the ratio of debt service to outstanding debt. The former is an indicator of the rollover process, expressing the proportion of loan disbursements used up by scheduled debt service payments during any period; the latter is a measure of loan terms.

The ratio of current account deficit to exports of goods and services is sometimes used, since the current account deficit broadly equals the full amount of new financing required. The current account deficit is divided by exports of goods and services, to adjust for the country's economic size.

Frank and Cline (1971) choose as a liquidity indicator the ratio of imports to reserves, where in subsequent studies the ratio of reserves to imports is used (Mayo and Barrett (1977), Cline (1984)). A country with larger reserves relative to imports is assumed to be unlikely to need debt rescheduling. The reserves/imports indicator can be expressed in months, i.e. the number of months for which the country can foot its import bill out of reserves. Country risk analysts tend to think that an "autonomy" of less than three months is grounds for concern, in that such a lack of liquidity may likely bring the country into debt problems.

The explanatory variable chosen by Solberg (1988) to represent the liquidity constraint on the borrowing country is the ratio of disbursed debt to international reserves. By comparing the stock magnitude of indebtedness to the current stock of reserves, this indicator measures the borrowing country's past reliance on external net capital flows *vis-à-vis* its prior foreign exchange savings. It is assumed to be positively correlated with the probability of rescheduling.

The ratio of imports to gross national product is adopted by some country risk analysts as a gauge of the degree to which national income growth will be affected if a country has to reduce its imports because of debt-servicing difficulties. A higher import/GNP ratio is said to indicate a higher probability of rescheduling, at least in the short run.

The export growth rate is sometimes used as an explanatory variable for debt rescheduling, since a country with rapid export growth is more likely to be earning the revenues required to service its debt.

Country risk analysts suggest that capital inflows should also be taken into account. The capital account indicator which appears in statistical studies is the ratio of capital inflows to debt service (or the inverse). Capital inflows represent part of the country's foreign exchange receipts used for servicing external debt. It is possible to assert the existence of a negative relationship between this ratio and the probability of a borrowing country's incurring debt servicing problems.

In some of the statistical analyses considered, variables that are indicators of the domestic economic situation also appear. These include *per capita* income and the rate of growth of *per capita* income. The former is an indicator of the standard of living. Higher income implies relatively greater consumption of non-essential items. This means that the government has greater flexibility in releasing resources for debt service payments and consequently a lower probability of default. Growth of *per capita* domestic product is seen as one of the most important factors affecting debt servicing capacity in the long run. Increased *per capita* output provides additional resources for debt service and increased consumption. Hence an increasing *per capita* product improves debt servicing capacity and lowers the probability of default.

There are also monetary variables indicating the effects of macroeconomic policy on the probability of rescheduling.

The money supply growth rate gives information about the monetary policy undertaken in a country. A high growth rate means rising prices which would make the country less competitive and cause balance of payments problems. The same negative effect on the balance of payments will be exerted by a high rate of inflation, a rapid growth of consumer price index and a high domestic credit/GDP ratio (which also indicates a "lax" monetary policy). The ratio of investment to national (or domestic) income is used by Kharas to give an idea of the importance placed on investment by the borrowing country. The higher the value of this ratio, the lower the probability of rescheduling. There is a negative relationship between the probability of rescheduling and the ratio of gross fixed capital formation to GDP, one of the indicators found significant by Mayo and Barrett (1977) and Solberg (1988). The explanation is that as a country devotes more of its resources to long-term investment it increases its productive capacity, thereby decreasing the likelihood of rescheduling.

Finally, a significant variable is relative purchasing power parity, introduced by Solberg (1988). This variable measures the debtor's global price competitiveness. An overvalued currency weakens export competitiveness and encourages import expenditures and capital flight. So a high purchasing power parity index worsens the debtor's medium term creditworthiness. There is, hence, a positive correlation between this variable and a country's rescheduling probability.

Table 1.2: Frank and Cline model

Authors of statistical model	Frank-Cline (1971)
Dependent variable	binary-valued: rescheduling, non rescheduling
Statistically significant explanatory variables	debt service ratio; imports/reserves; amortisation/debt
Method of analysis	discriminant analysis
Years of observation	1960–1968
Total number of observations	145
Total number of countries in the sample	26
Number of rescheduling cases	13 in 8 countries
Number of Type I errors	3
Error rate (number of error/number of obs.)	23%
Number of Type II errors	14
Error rate (number of error/number of obs.)	10.5%

Table 1.3: Dhonte model

Author of statistical model	Dhonte (1975)
Dependent variable	renegotiation of debt
Components	debt involvement; terms of the loan; size of debt service
Significant explanatory variables with respect to the first component	debt disbursements/imports; net transfers/ imports; debt outstanding/exports; debt outstanding/GNP
Significant explanatory variables with respect to the second component	debt service payments/debt disbursement; debt service payments/debt outstanding
Variables that help in distinguishing renegotiation cases	debt service/debt outstanding; debt service ratio; debt disbursement/imports
Method of analysis	principal components
Years of observation	1959–1971
Total number of observations	82
Number of rescheduling cases	13
Number of Type I errors	4
Error rate	34%
Number of Type II errors	9
Error rate	8%

Table 1.4: Grinols model

Author of statistical model	Grinols (1976)
Dependent variable	binary valued: rescheduling, non rescheduling
Statistically significant explanatory variables	debt service payments/reserves; disbursed external debt/debt service payments; debt service payments/imports; external debt/GDP; external debt/imports
Method of analysis	discrete analysis; discriminant analysis
Years of observation	1961–1974
Total number of observations	343
Total number of countries in the sample	64
Number of rescheduling cases	24
Number of Type I errors	3
Error rate	12.5%
Number of Type II errors	19
Error rate	6%

Table 1.5: Feder and Just model

Authors of statistical models	Feder-Just (1977)
Dependent variable	probability of default (rescheduling)
Statistically significant explanatory variables	debt service ratio; imports/reserves; amortisation/debt; *per capita* income; capital inflows/debt service payments; real export growth rate
Method of analysis	logit analysis
Years of observation	1962–1972
Total number of observations	238
Total number of countries in the sample	30
Number of rescheduling cases	21 in 11 countries
Number or Type I errors	1
Error rate	5%
Number of Type II errors	5
Error rate	2.5%

Table 1.6: Mayo and Barrett model

Authors of statistical model	Mayo and Barrett (1977)
Dependent variable	probability of rescheduling
Statistically significant explanatory variables	disbursed external debt/exports; reserves/ imports; gross fixed capital formation/GDP; imports/GDP; reserve position in IMF/imports; % change in consumer price index
Years of observation	1960–1975
Total number of observations	571
Total number of countries in the sample	48
Number of rescheduling cases	28
Number of Type I errors	7
Error rate	25%
Number of Type II errors	71
Error rate	13%

Table 1.7: Sargen model

Author of statistical model	Sargen (1977)
Dependent variable	binary valued: rescheduling, non rescheduling
Statistically significant explanatory variables	inflation rate; scheduled debt service payments/exports
Method of analysis	discriminant analysis
Years of observation	1960–1975
Total number of observations	466
Number of rescheduling cases	24
Number of Type I errors	8
Error rate	33%
Number of Type II errors	35
Error rate	8%

Table 1.8: Saini and Bates model

Authors of statistical model	Saini-Bates (1978)
Dependent variable	rescheduling + balance of payments support loans
Statistically significant explanatory variables	growth rate of consumer prices; money supply growth rate; adjusted cumulative current account balance/exports; growth rate of reserves
Methods of analysis	logit; discriminant
Years of observation	1960–1977
Total number of observations	298
Total number of countries in the sample	25
Number of rescheduling cases	23
Number of Type I errors	4
Error rate	17%
Number of Type II errors	42
Error rate	15%

Table 1.9: Abassi and Taffler model

Authors of statistical model	Abassi-Taffler (1982)
Dependent variable	rescheduling (voluntary rescheduling excluded)
Statistically significant explanatory variables	external debt/exports; commitment *per capita*; % change in consumer price index; domestic credit/GDP
Method of analysis	principal components
Years of observation	1967–1977
Total number of observations	681
Total number of countries in the sample	95
Number of rescheduling cases	55
Number of Type I errors	5
Error rate	10.5%
Number of Type II errors	56
Error rate	8.9%

Table 1.10: Kharas model

Author of the statistical method	Kharas (1984)
Dependent variable	need to reschedule
Statistically significant explanatory variables	debt service/GDP; capital inflows net of amortisation/GDP; population/GDP; investment/GDP
Method of analysis	probit analysis
Years of observation	1965–1976
Total number of observations	441
Number of rescheduling cases	30 (in 11 countries)
Number of Type I errors	5
Error rate	17%
Number of Type II errors	29
Error rate	7%

Table 1.11: Cline model

Author of statistical model	Cline (1984)
Dependent variable	probability of rescheduling
Statistically significant explanatory variables	debt service ratio; reserves/imports; amortisation; current account deficit/exports; rate of growth of *per capita* GDP; global external borrowing
Method of analysis	logit
Years of observations	1968–1982
Total number of observations	670
Number of countries in the sample	60
Number of rescheduling cases	22 in 15 countries
Number of Type I errors	2
Error rate	9.1%
Number of Type II errors	82
Error rate	13%

Table 1.12: Solberg model

Author of statistical model	Solberg (1988)
Dependent variable	probability of rescheduling
Statistically significant explanatory variables	imports/GDP; debt service ratio; incremental capital/output ratio; purchasing power parity; disbursed debt/international reserves
Methods of analysis	logit; probit
Years of observation	1971–1984
Total number of observations	770
Number of countries in the sample	67
Number of rescheduling cases	114 in 40 countries
Type I Error rate	18% Period 1971–1981
	29% Period 1982–1984
Type II Error rate	45% Period 1971–1981
	35% Period 1982–1984

1.5 FORECASTING POWER

The predictive ability of a statistical model is evaluated by seeing how many Type I and Type II errors are made when the model is used to forecast reschedulings subsequent to the sample years. It has often been held that statistical methods fail to predict reschedulings accurately.

The main problem in formulating predictions is making projections of the explanatory variables, as reliable forward data are generally not available for the developing countries.

As to the statistical methods just discussed, not all attempt to predict rescheduling cases.

In the pioneering model devised by Frank and Cline, predictions are formulated using the two-variable version (debt service ratio, debt amortisation/total debt outstanding) of their linear discriminant function. To be able to project the discriminant function, the authors made projections of total debt, interest payments, amortisation payments and debt service ratios for seventeen countries from 1967 to 1992. These projections proved to have a great many weaknesses: underestimation of debt service obligations, a predicted average annual export growth well under the actual one, and so forth.

Rather than try to predict the actual year of rescheduling, Frank and Cline computed the percentage of country years when a country was likely to encounter debt-servicing difficulties in the period 1967–1992.

Three groups of countries were identified. The first group consisted of "countries that were likely to be faced with serious debt servicing problems regardless of the aid assumption used or of the export growth rate". This group included India, Indonesia, Pakistan (countries which actually did conclude rescheduling agreements) and Tunisia (which did not).

The second group included Brazil, Chile, Colombia, the Dominican Republic, Israel, South Korea, Peru and Turkey, all these countries were predicted to reschedule, their export growth being low and their capital imports continuously growing. Turkey did not reschedule until after 1978 and Brazil not until 1983.

Countries belonging to group 3 were predicted not to encounter debt servicing difficulties under any conditions. To this group, according to Frank and Cline, belonged Mexico, Argentina, Bolivia, Iran and Nigeria. The predictions about countries belonging to group 3 produced four Type I errors, since all the cited countries but Iran rescheduled.

Feder and Just computed default probability predictions for 102 observations on public and publicly guaranteed loans granted to 27 developing countries during the 1973–1974 period. Only in the case of eight loans to three countries did the predicted probability of default exceed the default threshold of $P_R^* = 0.12$. Of this group of loans only three, for which the default probability prediction ranged from 0.82 to 0.89, were associated with a country reported to be seeking a rescheduling agreement. For the remaining five cases, one of the two models predicted default probabilities less than 0.18 for two observations, while the other model predicted probabilities higher than 0.5 for all five countries. Hence the authors concluded that for a critical threshold value, P_R^*, somewhere in the range from 0.18 to 0.50, three Type II errors were made using the first model (error rate = 3%) while five Type II errors (error rate = 4.9%) were made using the second model.

According to the authors the performance of the model could be judged as "good". However, the indirect testing procedure used and the small size of the sample makes it difficult to formulate straightforward judgments of Feder and Just's model predictive ability.

In Mayo and Barrett, the rescheduling group is defined in such a way as to include rescheduling up to five years later. That is, by the standards the authors use to assess the forecasting power of their early warning model a prediction of rescheduling is judged to be accurate if the country actually reschedules any time within five years. We should stress the difference with the other models cited, which propose to forecast reschedulings one year in advance. Moreover in their paper Mayo and Barrett do not attempt to formulate any ex ante prediction.

Dhonte and Kharas also attempt no prediction. A direct and straightforward predictive ability test is possible for the Abassi and Taffler model (1984) using the cases of rescheduling that took place in the period 1979–1983. In Abassi and Taffler, a country is predicted to reschedule in year $t+1$ if in year t it has a negative Z score. The model correctly predicted 50 of the 71 cases of rescheduling agreements undertaken in the 1979–1983 period. For the whole period, however, the model made a total of 83 Type II errors, i.e. cases where a predicted rescheduling failed to occur. According to the authors, the high Type II error rate is explicable in that 38 of the 83 errors referred to countries highly dependent on foreign capital; 21 referred to countries where rescheduling was postponed thanks to access to new foreign credit and four referred to countries characterized by political instability.

1.6 LIMITS OF STATISTICAL METHODS FOR COUNTRY RISK ANALYSIS

The main critiques usually addressed to statistical models of country risk assessment include: i) these models' neglect of social and political factors; ii) their failure to consider supply conditions in financial markets; iii) their downplaying of lenders' perception of creditworthiness; iv) their poor definition of the dependent variable; v) their problems of multicollinearity of independent variables; vi) their small data bases and inadequate number of dependent variable data sets; and vii) their lack of a well-defined theoretical foundation.

As to the first weakness, it is easily observed that the statistical methods we have briefly analyzed consider only economic circumstances that may lead to debt servicing difficulties. This is because often social and political factors are not easily quantifiable.

Turning to the second criticism, the only model that considers supply side factors is Cline (1984). The author makes it clear that a borrowing country may run into debt problems not only because of its "poor" performance but also because of a supply-side shock (like the general cutback in international lending that took place in 1982) or because on the basis of certain screening criteria lenders perceive the borrowing country as too risky to extend credit further.

The third problem relates to the use of rescheduling as a proxy for default on external debt. This choice may be judged inappropriate in light of the fact that options other than rescheduling are available to countries facing debt servicing difficulties. Debt refinancing and restructuring, balance-of-payments support loans and debt service delays, for example, are good substitutes for rescheduling.

Moreover Hefferman, Delmain and Hollist (1985) note that rescheduling cannot always be considered a "bad event" for the lender. Sometimes even in the presence of a rescheduling agreement a lender may experience a net present value gain. And they say: "This throws into doubt the purpose of the statistical studies that attempt to identify the variables crucial to rescheduling as if the event would prove to be an unprofitable one for the lender."

Furthermore, the cause-and-effect chain implied by statistical models, which run from changes in the economic variables to the probability of default may not actually be so straightforward. The response of lenders to a perceived increase in the probability of rescheduling may well affect the economic variables, which in turn influence the probability of rescheduling. If this is the case, methods of simultaneous estimation should be used. The problem of multicollinearity (or lack of independence between independent variables) is again stressed by Hefferman (1986). Some method to correct for the multicollinearity present in a model (such as varimax rotation) should be used if required, and in any case a careful selection of dependent variables may help.

The small size of the sample is especially relevant to the sample of rescheduling cases. For purposes of estimation, these simply do not form a large enough set. The use of panel data may be of some help in solving this problem.

The most serious problem, however, in my own view, is the lack of theoretical foundations. The need to analyse the determinants of the demand and supply of foreign loans in a general theoretical framework and then to understand why debt servicing problems may arise is the object of study of the next part of this book.

1.7 COUNTRY RANKINGS OF *EUROMONEY* AND *INSTITUTIONAL INVESTOR*

Before studying of the determinants of foreign loan demand and supply, let us spend a few lines to describe how two leading financial reviews, *Euromoney* and *Institutional Investor,* rank borrowing countries according to their perceived creditworthiness. *Euromoney* presents an annual Country Risk League Table consisting of a ranking of countries that have borrowed on the Eurocurrency market compiled on the basis of the weighted average spread (over the London Interbank offered rate (LIBOR)) they were able to obtain. The higher the spread, the less creditworthy the country and the higher its ranking in the league table.

It has been noted, however (Abassi and Taffler (1982), Heffernan (1986)) that this method of creditworthiness assessment has some shortcomings. First of all, a country can be rated only if it borrows on the Eurocurrency market and only on the basis of the loan it has negotiated. Secondly, considering the spread over LIBOR as the only means of credit rationing is a bit myopic, since fees may also act as a good substitute for higher spreads.

Since autumn 1982, the way *Euromoney* computes the country ranking has changed; three factors are now considered in assessing how risky a country is and different weights are assigned to the factors. The first element is ease of access to all international capital markets. To this element a weight of 40 per cent is assigned. The other two factors, weighted at 30 per cent each, are the terms a country obtains in the syndicated loan market and the relative success of syndication.

Institutional Investor also produces a creditworthiness table, published twice a year in March and September. The *Institutional Investor* Credit Rating system is based on the results of a survey in which 75–100 banks are asked to grade the creditworthiness of each country on a scale of 0 (most chance of default) to 100 (least chance of default). No bank ranks the country in which it has its headquarters. The individual responses are then weighted according to an undisclosed formula that "...properly gives more weight to responses from banks with the largest worldwide lending exposure and the most sophisticated country analysis systems" (*Institutional Investor,* September 1980). The ranking includes developed countries and also those which have not borrowed on the Eurocurrency market.

A critique that may be addressed to the *Institutional Investor* Rating System is that the banker's judgment will always include a subjective element. Moreover some bias might be brought in by the assignment of heavier weights to highly exposed banks. In fact, often sovereign lending by a bank tends to be concentrated in one country or geographical area – hence, the expertise of the bank that has the heavier weight does not usually extend to all the countries included in the ranking.

2 The supply of foreign loans

It has been claimed that banks have been reckless in the extension of loans to developing countries. It is thus important to understand the criteria according to which suppliers formulate their lending decisions.

We know that in developing its asset portfolio a bank is concerned with many factors, such as the expected return on loans, the risk, the front-end and other fee-income associated with its credits, the value of other business relationships which are generated by extending various credits, political considerations, and the maturity of matching assets and liabilities.

The bank's objective will depend on the factor it is primarily interested in. If the rate of return on assets is the primary yardstick, the bank will arrange the composition of its portfolio so as to maximize the overall expected return.

In the theory of finance, concerning optimal portfolio choice, two types of risk are identified: unsystematic or diversifiable risk and systematic or nondiversifiable risk. Unsystematic risk is associated with factors affecting individual asset returns and can be reduced through diversification. Systematic risk, on the other hand, is associated with factors affecting all assets in the market and is therefore not diversifiable.

If systematic risk is the only risk a bank is concerned with, it should choose the composition of its portfolio so as to maximize expected return adjusted for the degree of systematic risk and should ignore the variability of returns on individual loans and the correlation between returns on different loans. The adjustment of expected return for systematic risk is discussed in section 2.4, below.

If, on the other hand, a bank is solely concerned with total risk, its objective will be the minimization of risk through diversification.

It is likely, however, for bank managers to be concerned with both expected return and risk, trying to maximize expected return for a given amount of risk or to minimize risk for a given expected return.

It has also been suggested that the relevant distinction from the point of view of a bank involved in foreign banking activities, is between market (or systematic) risk and bankruptcy risk (Shapiro, 1982). The risk of banks going bankrupt is related to total earnings variability, but now the bank's objective is the minimization of the probability of bankruptcy instead of the minimization of the variance of overall return.

In the following sections we analyse how to derive a bank's optimal portfolio of foreign loan assets under different assumptions about its objective.

2.1 BASIC ASSUMPTIONS

There are two assets (or portfolios of assets) available for investment: a domestic asset, D, and a foreign asset, F.

The portfolio's return, expected return and variance of return are respectively given by

$$Rp = x_1 R_D + x_2 R_F \quad (1)$$

$$E(Rp) = x_1 E(R_D + x_2 E(R_F) \quad (2)$$

$$\sigma_R^2 = [x_1^2 \sigma_D^2 + x_2^2 \sigma_F^2 + 2x_1 x_2 \sigma_{DF}] \quad (3)$$

$$= [x_1^2 \sigma_D^2 + x_2^2 \sigma_F^2 + 2x_1 x_2 p \sigma_D \sigma_F] \quad (4)$$

where

R_D, R_F = net returns on domestic and foreign assets

x_1, x_2 = fraction of bank's capital committed to domestic and foreign assets

σ_D^2, σ_F^2 = variances of return on domestic and foreign assets

σ_{DF} = covariance between the return on domestic assets and the return on foreign assets

$p = \dfrac{\sigma_{DF}}{\sigma_D \sigma_F}$ is the correlation coefficient

E = expectation of

Banks are assumed to operate in a perfectly competitive environment, to act with respect to assets as quantity setters and to face a single period problem.

No reserve requirement or capital to asset ratio is imposed by regulatory authorities. Banks' capital is assumed to be a fixed amount, and to simplify analysis it is set equal to 1.

2.2 THE MAXIMIZATION OF OVERALL EXPECTED RETURN ON PORTFOLIO

If banks are not concerned with risk and care only about return, they will construct their portfolio so as to maximize expected return or the expected utility of the return.

The maximization problem faced by the bank is

$$\text{maximize} \quad E(Rp)$$

$$\text{subject to} \quad x_1 + x_2 = 1$$

where the overall portfolio expected return, $E(Rp)$ is given by equation (2).

The solution to the maximization problem suggests that if we want the bank to have a diversified portfolio, the yields on the two types of asset must have the same mathematical expectation.

The proportion of capital held in domestic and in foreign assets, however, is indeterminate, since the bank is indifferent between them. If, on the other hand, the expected return on the domestic asset is higher than the expected return on the foreign asset, all capital will be held in the domestic asset and the supply of foreign loans will disappear.

2.3 THE MINIMIZATION OF RISK AND THE SUPPLY OF LOANS TO DEVELOPING COUNTRIES

If a bank instead of looking at expected return is concerned with total risk, it will proportion the domestic and foreign assets in its portfolio so as to minimize the variance of the overall portfolio return.

As was shown in equation 2 the expected return on a portfolio is determined by the expected return of each of the underlying assets weighted by their share in the portfolio.

By contrast, the variance of return on a portfolio (equation 3) depends not only upon the variance of the individual assets, but also on the extent to which the rates of return on assets move together.

The value of x_1 that minimizes $\sigma^2(Rp)$ is

$$x_1 = \frac{\sigma_F^2 - \sigma_{DF}}{\sigma_D^2 + \sigma_F^2 - 2\sigma_{DF}} \qquad (5)$$

and the corresponding value for x_2, $x_2 = 1 - x_1$, is

$$x_1 = \frac{\sigma_D^2 - \sigma_{DF}}{\sigma_D^2 + \sigma_F^2 - 2\sigma_{DF}} \qquad (6)$$

A sufficient condition for x_1 to be an interior point (ie. $0 < x_1 < 1$) and thus to yield a global minimum is $\sigma_D^2, \sigma_F^2 > \sigma_{DF}$

The proportion of net worth committed to foreign assets (hence the supply of foreign loans) depends on the variances of domestic and foreign returns and on their covariance. More precisely x_2 is an increasing function of σ_D^2,

$$\frac{\delta x_2}{\delta \sigma_D^2} > 0$$

and a decreasing function of σ_F^2,

$$\frac{\delta x_2}{\delta \sigma_F^2} < 0$$

if the condition $\sigma_D^2, \sigma_F^2 > \sigma_{DF}$ holds.

The effect of the covariance between returns on the supply of foreign loans depends on the difference between the two variances $\sigma_D{}^2 - \sigma_F{}^2$,

$$\frac{\delta x_2}{\delta \sigma_{DF}} = \frac{\sigma_D^2 - \sigma_F^2}{\sigma_D^2 + \sigma_F^2 - 2\sigma_{DF}}$$

If the variance of the return on domestic assets is greater (smaller) than the variance of return on foreign assets then there will be a positive (negative) relation between the proportion of the bank's capital committed to foreign assets and the covariance between the two returns.

2.4 THE BANK'S OBJECTIVE WHEN THE RELEVANT NOTION OF RISK IS SYSTEMATIC RISK

However, as noted, total risk can be partitioned into two parts: systematic risk, which is a measure of how an asset (or a portfolio of assets) covaries with the economy, and unsystematic risk, which is independent of the economy.

It has been suggested that since it is possible to diversify away any asset specific risk[1] banks should be concerned only with systematic risk.

It follows that a bank should concentrate on maximizing expected return adjusted for the degree of systematic risk. To this end it should first derive a measure of risk for each individual asset.

From the Capital Asset Pricing Model (CAPM) we know that, since the asset market is the sum of all individual holdings, the market portfolio, in equilibrium, consists of all marketable assets held according to their market value weights.[2]

It follows that a measure of the risk associated with asset i is given by

$$\beta_i = \frac{\sigma_{im}}{\sigma_m^2} = \frac{\mathrm{cov}(R_i, R_m)}{\mathrm{var}(R_m)} \tag{7}$$

where R_i is the return on asset i, R_m is the return on the market portfolio, σ_{im} is the covariance between the return on asset i and the return on market portfolio and σ_m^2 the variance of the return on market portfolio.

Since an important property of this measure of risk for individual assets is that it is linearly additive when the assets are combined into portfolios, the β of a portfolio consisting of x_1 of capital invested in domestic asset, D and of x_2 of capital invested in foreign asset, F is

$$\beta_p = x_1\beta_D + x_2\beta_F \tag{8}$$

The expression for portfolio expected return adjusted for systematic risk is given by

$$E(Rp) = R_z + [\, E(R_m) - R_z\,]\, \beta_p \tag{9}$$

where R_z is the return on a risk-free asset and the term $[(E(R_m) - R_z)]\beta_p$ is the risk premium obtained multiplying the price of risk, $[E(R_m) - R_z]$, by the quantity of risk β_p.

Actually in equilibrium the price of risk is the marginal rate of substitution between risk and return and equals the slope of the capital market line.

$$\text{Equilibrium price of risk} = \text{MRS}_{\sigma_R}^{E(Rp)} = \frac{E(R_m) - R_z}{\sigma_m}$$

and the quantity of risk is

$$\frac{\text{cov}(Rp, R_m)}{\sigma_m}$$

But since the standard deviation of the market, σ_m, is assumed to be constant, risk is given by β_p and the price of risk by $E(R_m) - R_z$.

What equation 9 says is that the portfolio rate of return is equal to the risk-free rate of return plus a risk premium. When the relevant notion of risk is systematic risk, the bank's objective becomes to maximize expected return as given by equation 9.

2.5 THE MINIMIZATION OF THE PROBABILITY OF BANKRUPTCY AS AN ALTERNATIVE OBJECTIVE

It has been suggested that bank managers, instead of being concerned with risk as represented by the overall variance of return, are actually concerned with the possibility of the bank going bankrupt (Shapiro, 1982). If this is exclusively so, the bank's objective becomes minimizing the risk, or the probability, of bankruptcy.

Following Shapiro (1982), bankruptcy is defined as losses in excess of the bank's capital. The bank will consequently go bankrupt if the losses, $(-Rp)$, are greater than the bank's capital which by assumption is equal to 1:

$$\begin{aligned} \text{probability of bankruptcy} &= \text{probability of } -Rp > 1 \\ &= \text{probability of } Rp < -1 \end{aligned} \tag{10}$$

To derive a measure of the probability of bankruptcy we use Chebyshev's inequality.

Since Rp is a random variable with mean $E(Rp)$ and variance $\sigma^2(Rp)$, according to Chebyshev's inequality[3] we can write

$$Pr\ (\mid Rp - E(Rp)\mid)\ \geq\ E(Rp) + 1)\ \leq\ \frac{\sigma_R^2}{(E(Rp) + 1)^2} \tag{11}$$

Moreover the probability that [Rp – $E(Rp)$] will assume values outside the interval [$-E(Rp)$ –1, $E(Rp)$ +1] is equal to the sum of the probabilities referring to two incompatible events:

$$Pr\ (\mid Rp - E(Rp)\mid)\ \geq\ E(Rp) + 1)$$

$$= Pr(Rp \leq -1) + Pr(Rp \geq 2E(Rp) + 1) \tag{12}$$

Combining equations (11) and (12) we get

$$Pr\ (Rp \leq\ -1)\ \leq\ \frac{\sigma_R^2}{(E(Rp) + 1)^2}\ -\ Pr(Rp \geq 2E(Rp) + 1) \tag{13}$$

But if equation 13 is true, it is certainly true that

$$Pr\ (Rp \leq\ -1)\ \leq\ \frac{\sigma_R^2}{(E(Rp) + 1)^2} \tag{14}$$

where $E(Rp)$ and σ_R^2 are given by equation (2) and (3) respectively.

Substituting (6) and (7) into equation (15) we get

$$Pr(Rp \leq 1)\ \leq\ \frac{x_1^2\sigma_D^2 + x_2^2\sigma_F^2 + 2x_1x_2\sigma_{DF}}{[x_1E(R_D) + x_2E(R_F) + 1]^2} \tag{15}$$

Now the bank chooses x_1 and x_2 to minimize the risk of bankruptcy as given by equation (14).

This occurs for

$$x_1^* = \frac{[\sigma_F^2E(R_D) + 1) - \sigma_{DF}(E(R_F) + 1)}{\sigma_D^2E(R_F) + \sigma_F^2E(R_D) - \sigma_{DF}[E(R_D) + E(R_F) + 2]} \tag{16}$$

and

$$x_2^* = \frac{[\sigma_D^2E(R_F) + 1) - \sigma_{DF}(E(R_D) + 1)}{\sigma_D^2E(R_F) + \sigma_F^2E(R_D) - \sigma_{DF}[E(R_D) + E(R_F) + 2]} \tag{17}$$

According to equation (17) x_2^*, the fraction of bank capital committed to foreign assets, and hence the supply of loans to developing countries, is a decreasing function of σ_F^2 and $E(R_D)$ and an increasing function of σ_D^2 and $E(R_F)$.

2.6 APPLYING THE MEAN-VARIANCE APPROACH

Next we consider the case in which banks are concerned with both risk and return and apply the mean-variance approach to describe suppliers' behaviour. We first postulate that the probability distribution of portfolio returns is normal. We assume further that for a given value of its capital and of the variance of portfolio return, each bank prefers more expected portfolio return to less and for a given value of its capital and portfolio return, it prefers less standard deviation of portfolio return to more.

The assumption that portfolio return distributions are normal and that banks like expected returns and dislike the standard deviation of return imply that the bank's portfolio can be classified as optimal or efficient if it has the property that no other portfolio with an equally high expected return has lower standard deviation.

We first derive the set of efficient portfolios.

First note that the investor may choose to have a diversified portfolio, to hold only foreign assets, or to hold only domestic assets.

If the bank decides to hold only domestic assets, $x_1 = 1$ and $x_2 = 0$. Point *D* in Figure 1 gives the combination of $E(Rp)$ and σ_R that correspond to $x_1 = 1, x_2 = 0$.

Alternatively the bank can commit all its capital to foreign assets. Point F in figure 1 corresponds to the combination of expected return and risk where all funds are invested in foreign assets.

As for diversified portfolios holding both types of assets, we should look at the relationship between expected return and risk for different values of the correlation coefficient.

With perfect positive correlation between returns, any value of x_1 between 0 and 1 generates a combination of $E(Rp)$ and σ_R along the straight line between *D* and *F* in Figure 2.1.

Figure 2.1
The relationship between expected return and risk with perfect positive correlation between the two assets

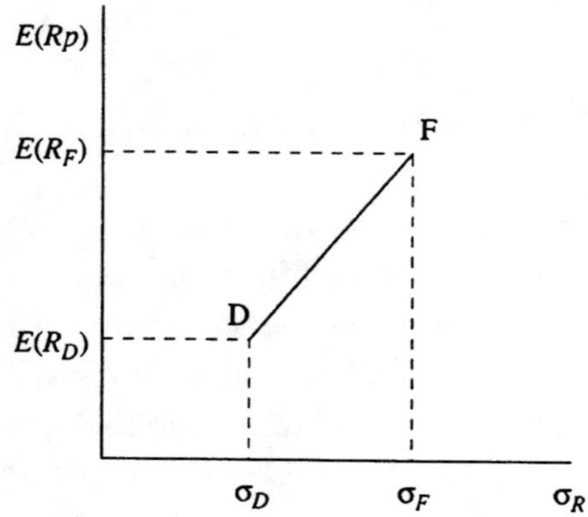

This is so because when $p = 1$,

$$\sigma_R = x_1\sigma_D + x_2\sigma_F \tag{18}$$

or, since $x_1 = 1 - x_2$,

$$\sigma_R = \sigma_D + x_2\,(\sigma_F - \sigma_D) \tag{19}$$

and the relationship between expected return and risk becomes

$$E(Rp) \;=\; E(R_D) + \frac{\sigma_R - \sigma_D}{\sigma_F - \sigma_D}\,[E(R_F - E(R_D)] \tag{20}$$

With perfect negative correlation, p = –1, the standard deviation becomes

$$\begin{aligned}\sigma_R &= [x_1^2\sigma_D^2 + x_2^2\sigma_F^2 - 2x_1x_2\sigma_D\sigma_F]^{1/2} \\ &= |\,x_1\sigma_D - x_2\sigma_F\,| \end{aligned} \tag{21}$$

Given x_1, $0 < x_1 < 1$, and given values of σ_D and σ_F, perfect negative correlation gives the smallest possible value of σ_R.

At the extreme, perfect negative correlation with both x_1 and x_2 strictly positive implies the existence of a portfolio composed of a domestic asset, *D*, and of a foreign asset, *F*, which has zero standard deviation of return.

From equation 19 it follows that

$$\sigma_R = 0 \text{ when } x_1 = \frac{\sigma_F}{\sigma_D + \sigma_F} \tag{22}$$

$$\sigma_R = x_1\,\sigma_D - x_2\,\sigma_F \text{ when } x_1 > \frac{\sigma_F}{\sigma_D + \sigma_F} \tag{23}$$

$$\sigma_R = x_2\,\sigma_F - x_1\,\sigma_D \text{ when } x_1 > \frac{\sigma_F}{\sigma_D + \sigma_F} \tag{24}$$

When $x_1 = 1$ we are at point D in figure 2.

Figure 2.2
The relationship between expected return and risk with perfect positive and perfect negative correlation between the two assets

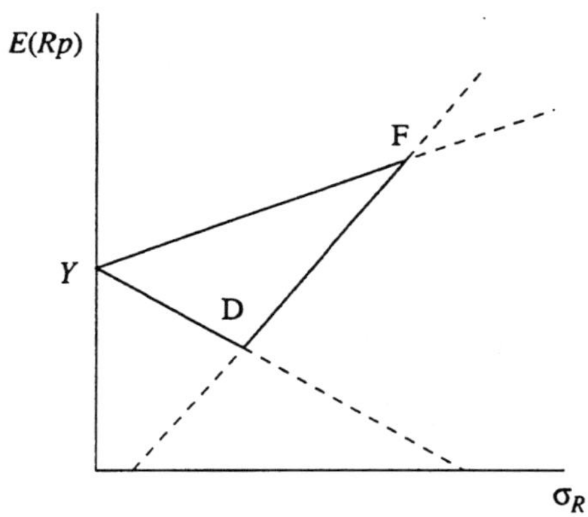

For $1 > x > \dfrac{\sigma_F}{\sigma_D + \sigma_F}$

the combinations of $E(R\text{p})$ and σ_F obtained are described by equations (2) and (23) and in Figure 2.2 we move away from D along a straight line that intersects the $E(Rp)$ axis at y.

For $\quad 1 > x < \dfrac{\sigma_F}{\sigma_D + \sigma_F}$

the combinations of $E(R)$ and σ_R obtained are described by equations (2) and (24) and in Figure 2.2 we move along the other straight line away from y in direction of point F which is reached when $x_1 = 0$ and $x_2 = 1$.

Given x_1, $0 < x_1 < 1$, and given values of σ_D^2 and σ_F^2 the maximum value for σ_R occurs when R_D and R_F are perfectly positively correlated, while the minimum value for σ_R occurs when R_D and R_F are perfectly negatively correlated.

With less than perfect positive correlation, $p < 1$,

$$\sigma_R < |x_1\sigma_D + x_2\sigma_F| \tag{25}$$

where $x_1\sigma_D + x_2\sigma_F$ is the value of σ_R for $p = 1$.

The relationship between the risk and the proportion of assets in the portfolio is no longer linear.[4]

Moreover σ_R decreases as p decreases (see Figure 2.3).

Figure 2.3
The relationship between the risk and the proportion of assets in the portfolio

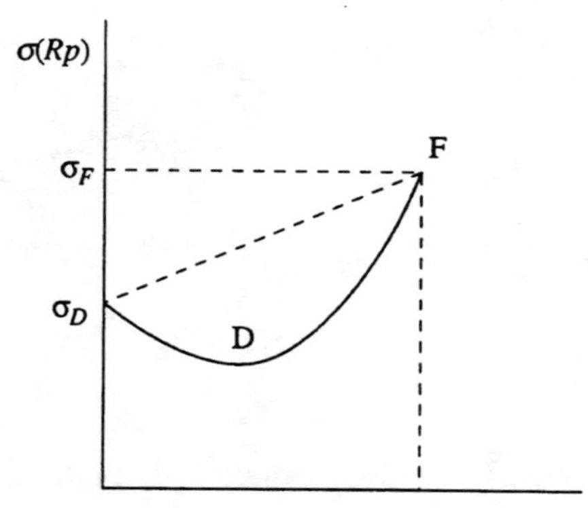

When $-1 < p < 1$ the combinations of $E(Rp)$ and σ_R obtained by varying x between 1 and 0 form a curve between points D and F.

The curve must be to the left of the line between D and F describing the combinations of $E(Rp)$ and σ_R obtained when $p = 1$ and to the right of the two line segments that describe the combinations of $E(Rp)$ and σ_R obtained with perfect negative correlation between R_D and R_F.

In short, with less than perfect correlation, the combinations of D and F must be along a line somewhat like DF where each positively sloped segment of the curve must be concave and any negatively sloped segment must be convex (Figure 2.4).

Figure 2.4
The relationship between expected return and risk for all possible values of the correlation coefficient

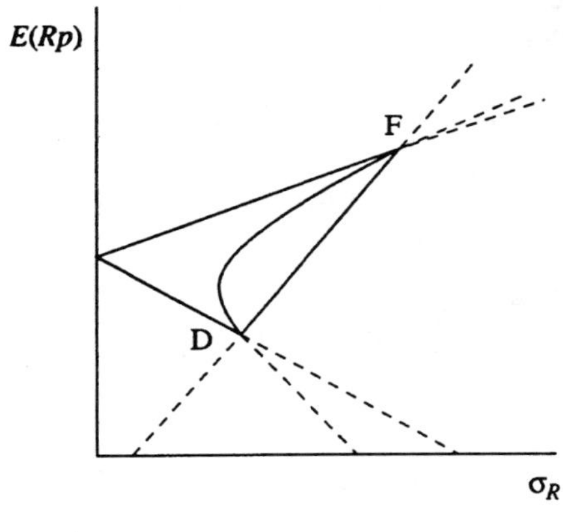

Moreover for our analysis it is important to note that when there is less than perfect positive correlation between the returns on the two assets (or portfolios), D and F, diversification is an effective way to reduce dispersion and, hence, risk. Now, if we assume that there is no short selling and no free lending or borrowing; that there are no feasible portfolios with $\sigma_R = 0$; that there are no portfolios on the boundary whose returns are perfectly positively correlated, the feasible set of portfolios is the one represented in Figure 2.5.

Figure 2.5
The feasible set of portfolios

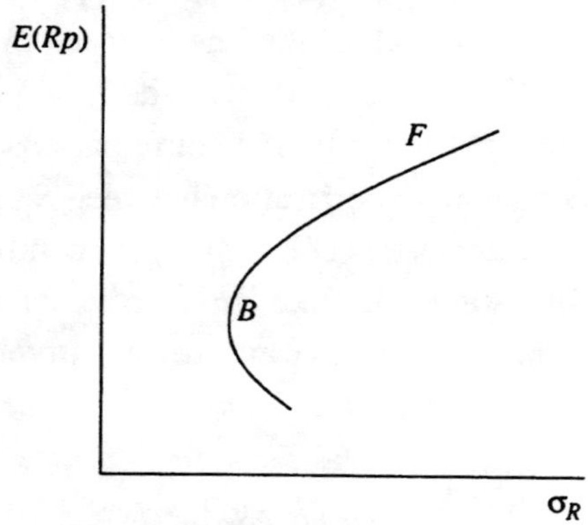

The portfolios that minimize σ_R at a given level of *E*(*Rp*) are called minimum variance portfolios.

In geometric terms, the set of minimum variance portfolios is the left boundary of the feasible set of portfolios. That is, minimum variance portfolios are those that are as close as possible to the *E*(*Rp*) axis at each feasible level of *E*(*Rp*).

Efficient portfolios are minimum variance portfolios, but not all minimum variance portfolios are efficient.

The efficient portfolios in Figure 2.5 are those along the left boundary above point *B*. Thus the segment *BF* is the set of efficient portfolios (Figure 2.6).

Figure 2.6
The set of efficient portfolios

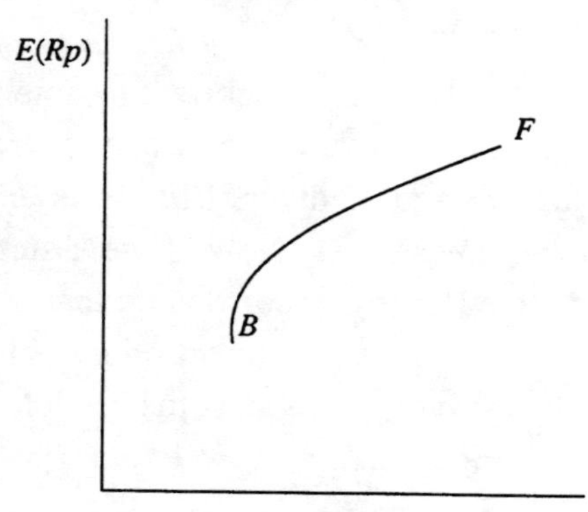

Let us now introduce the bank's tastes for expected return and standard deviation of return.

These can be represented by a continuous utility function U defined for all ($E(R)$, σ_R) such that:

- U is increasing in $E(Rp)$ and decreasing in σ_R
- U is strictly quasi-concave since we are assuming that investors are risk-adverse

We then obtain a family of indifference curves like the one represented in Figure 2.7.

Figure 2.7

The bank's testes for expected return and standard deviation of return

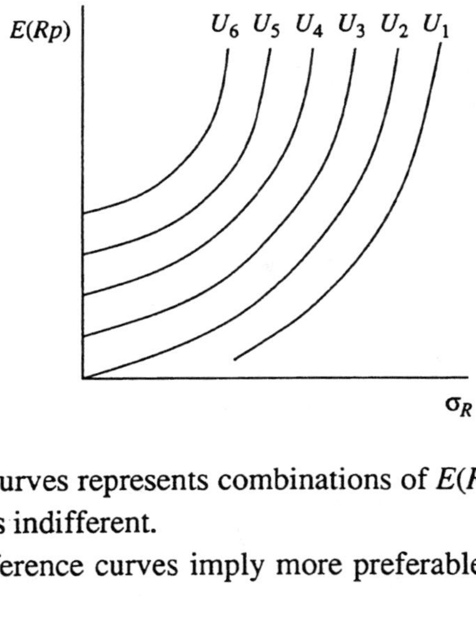

Each of the curves represents combinations of $E(Rp)$ and σ_R among which the bank is indifferent.

Higher indifference curves imply more preferable combinations of $E(Rp)$ and σ_R.

Formally the problem for the bank is

$$\text{maximize} \quad U(E(Rp), \sigma_R)$$

$$\text{subject to} \quad E(Rp)=x_1E(R_1)+x_2E(R_2)$$

$$\sigma_R = [x_1^2\sigma_D^2 + x_2^2\sigma_F^2+2x_1x_2\sigma_{DF}]^{1/2}.$$

The assumptions on the utility function imply that a solution to this problem exists and is unique.

This solution is illustrated in Figure 2.8.

Figure 2.8
The solution to the maximization problem fronted by banks

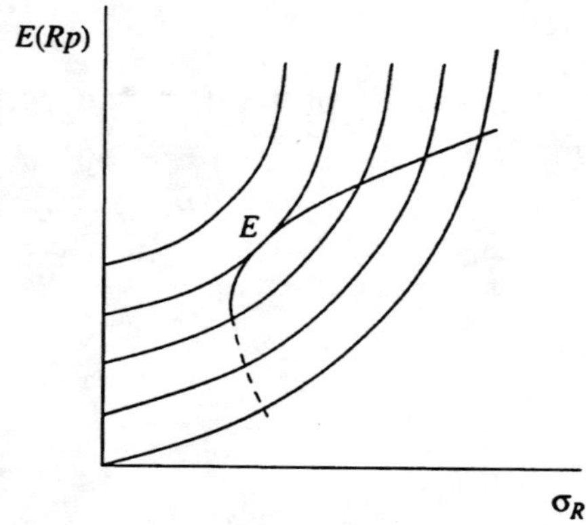

The optimal efficient loan portfolio chosen by the bank is the one that puts it on the highest attainable indifference curve.

2.7 THE SUPPLY OF FOREIGN LOANS WHEN THE BANK'S UTILITY FUNCTION IS A QUADRATIC APPROXIMATION

Focusing on the mean and variance can also be justified if we assume that a bank has a utility function $U(Rp)$ defined in the return, and we utilize a quadratic approximation.[5]

$$U\,(Rp) = U(0) + Rp\;U'(0) + \frac{U''(0)R^2}{2} \tag{26}$$

Expected utility yielded is

$$E(U)=U(0) + U'(0)E(Rp) + \frac{U''(0)}{2}\,[\sigma_R^2 + E(Rp)^2] \tag{27}$$

The values of x_1 and x_2 that maximize $E(U)$ are

$$x_1 = \frac{(c - E(R_F))(E(R_D) - E(R_F)) + \sigma_F^2 - \sigma_{DF}}{[(E(R_D) - E(R_F))^2 + \sigma_D^2 + \sigma_F^2 - 2\sigma_{DF}]} \tag{28}$$

$$x_2 = \frac{(c - E(R_D))(E(R_F) - E(R_D)) + \sigma_D^2 - \sigma_{DF}}{[(E(R_D) - E(R_F))^2 + \sigma_D^2 + \sigma_F^2 - 2\sigma_{DF}]} \tag{29}$$

where $c = \frac{U''(0)}{U'(0)}$ is the coefficient of absolute risk aversion of U and where if the quadratic approximation of U is to be well behaved (ie. $\frac{\delta E(U)}{\delta E(R)} > 0$) we need $c - E(R_F)$ and $c - E(R_D) > 0$.

x_2 can be interpreted as the supply of foreign loans and, as it can be seen in equation (29), it depends on the difference between expected returns, on the two variances, on the covariance and on the coefficient of absolute risk aversion.

2.8 THE TRADE-OFF BETWEEN EXPECTED RETURN AND BANKRUPTCY RISK

If instead of speaking about risk as represented by the variance of portfolio return we assume that the risk the bank cares about is the risk of insolvency then the relevant trade-off is between expected return and bankruptcy risk.

One possible way of expressing this trade-off (Shapiro, 1982) is to write a bank's expected utility as

$$E(U) = E(Rp) - \alpha K \tag{30}$$

where α is the probability of bankruptcy as given by equation (14) and K the cost of bankruptcy.

The bank now chooses x_1 and x_2 to maximize $E(U)$ where

$$E(U) = E(Rp) - \frac{\sigma_R^2}{[E(Rp) + 1]^2} K \tag{31}$$

subject to the constraint

$$x_1 + x_2 = 1$$

This is done by setting

$$\frac{\delta U}{\delta x_1} = 0$$

$$\frac{\delta U}{\delta x_2} = 0$$

and solving for x_1 and x_2.

2.9 THE APPLICABILITY OF PORTFOLIO THEORY TO BANKS' LOAN PORTFOLIOS

There are a number of factors limiting the applicability of conventional portfolio theory to bank loan portfolios.

The problems arise, first of all, because the measurement of risk and return on loans is difficult.

Measuring the expected return is difficult because lending contracts are complex and because many different sources of profits may be implicitly tied together within a customer relationship .

Two important components of expected return are the repayment of principal and the interest return, usually defined as the spread over the three-month or six-month LIBOR, or some similar floating base rate of interest. But principal and interest return are only the most obvious components of expected return.

In the case of agents involved in international loan syndication, there is a share of fees agreed upon with the borrower. These may be quite high, and if in excess of the incremental costs involved in providing syndication services may add to the overall return of banks involved in syndicate management. In other cases banks may lend to a particular borrower at unattractive terms in order to develop or maintain a "relationship" that may generate future earning from a variety of activities or to establish relationships with third parties involving additional future return. Expected return, then, is composed of many elements and each element has its own time profile and expected value.

As to risk, its direct estimation based on the historical performance of loans is no easy matter since, in most cases, loans perform according to contract with comparatively little observable variation.

As an alternative to reviewing historical movements, the riskiness of a loan is often inferred using current financial data on the borrower in conjunction with available information. The risk assessment procedures developed, however, do not focus directly on the problem of measuring the covariances of risk across different countries, a key requirement for the construction of efficient portfolios.

Another problem with the application of modern portfolio theory to banks' loan portfolios is that the principal and interest components of expected return in loan portfolios may be subject to asymmetrical variance: that is the variance of these returns may be entirely on the down-side. The return distribution will then look very much like a truncated distribution, whereas one of the basic assumptions of portfolio theory is that the distribution of expected returns is normal.

2.10 MEASURING RISK

A possible application of portfolio theory to bank loans is given by Goodman (1981). Goodman observes that since the figures for rates of return on foreign loans are not available and consequently it is not possible to estimate risk in a portfolio of domestic and LDC credits, one must rely on proxies related to rates of return. In her article, she chooses proxies that capture country risk considerations.

As mentioned in Chapter 1, proxies for country risk may be found in indicators of problems that may affect a country's ability to repay its debts, such as: balance-of-payments difficulties caused by real or monetary disturbances, liquidity difficulties and political difficulties. Each of these types of difficulty could be expected in some instances to translate into a difference between the actual and promised rate of return.

The proxies chosen for country risk are:

(1) growth of exports
(2) growth of money supply
(3) growth of international reserves
(4) growth of imports/reserves

The growth-of-exports proxy measures balance-of-payments risk due to real disturbances; the growth of the money supply serves as a proxy for balance-of-payments difficulties due to monetary risk; and the final two measures serve as proxies for liquidity risk.

Moreover, as we have seen, the actual rate of return on an asset may be separated into two components: one that is asset-specific and independent of all other returns (the non-systematic component) and another that is common to all assets (the systematic component).

Consequently we can assume that the rate of return on an asset is linearly related to both the market rate of return and an asset-specific factor

$$R_i = a_i + b_i L + C_i \qquad (32)$$

where R_i is the actual return on asset i, a_i and b_i are two constants, L is the actual return of an index comprised of all relevant assets and C_i is an uncertain variable (representing market return) related to asset-specific factors.

The variance of an individual asset, also, can be separated into a systematic component consisting of background factors, which affect all assets, and a non-systematic component. The variance of a portfolio, then, takes on the simple form:

$$\sigma^2{}_p = b^2\sigma_t^2 + x_1^2\sigma_{c1}^2 + x_2^2\sigma_{c2}^2 + \ldots x_N{}^2\sigma_{c2}^2 \qquad (33)$$

where

$$b = \sum b_i Xi \qquad i = 1, \ldots. \mathrm{N}$$

and N is the number of assets in the portfolio.

It is then possible to divide each proxy into its systematic and non-systematic component and estimate risk.

Starting from a regression performed for each country:

$$X_i = a_i + b_i\ \bar{X} + e \qquad (34)$$

where X_i is the risk measure for country i

$\bar{X}$ is the index constructed for each proxy from the country indices, with each country weighted by its borrowing share

a_i and b_i are constants

e_i is the error term.

The systematic variance for country i, for a given risk measure, is equal to the square of the b_i constant obtained from the regression multiplied by the variance of the index:

systematic variance: $b_i^2\,\sigma_x^2$

The non-systematic variance is the square of the standard error of the regression multiplied by $(N-2)/(N)$:

non-systematic variance =
(standard error of regression)$^2(N-2)/(N)$

This approach allows for a quantification of diversifiable and non-diversifiable risk when there are no reliable rate-of-return measures.

2.11 STATE PREFERENCE THEORY

In conclusion, the application of modern portfolio theory to bank loan portfolios is problematic in a number of ways:

- it is difficult to measure the risks and returns associated with certain types of loans, in particular foreign loans;
- there is an asymmetry in bank lending, arising from a limited upside on expected return.

It has accordingly been proposed (Heffernan 1985) to apply state preference theory to the derivation of the lender's optimal loan portfolio.

State preference theory is a variant of expected utility theory.

The objects on which lender's preference ordering is defined are the pure claims to wealth W_a and W_b, and the lender makes his choice so as to maximize expected utility defined as:

$$E(U) = \pi_a U_a(W_a) + \pi_b U_b(W_b) \tag{35}$$

where π_a and π_b are the subjective probabilities the lender attaches to the occurrence of states *a* and *b* and $U_a(W_a)$ and $U_b(W_b)$ are the utilities derived respectively from holding claims to wealth W_a if state *a* obtains and claims to wealth W_b if state *b* obtains.

For simplicity it is usually assumed that there are only two states of the world and that there is a single wealth utility function independent of the state in which the wealth is enjoyed. The investor chooses how to divide wealth between different assets so as to maximize the expected utility of claims to wealth.

Following Heffernan (1985) we now assume that there are two assets from which to choose: a safe asset which yields r_s and a risky asset – a sovereign loan to a developing country – with an associate yield of r_F

The sovereign loan is perceived as risky by the lender because there is a positive probability of default.

The two states are defined as a good state, which obtains when the sovereign loan is entirely repaid on time, and a bad state, when only part of the total obligation is met.

The claims to wealth associated with the good state and the bad state are respectively given by

$$Y_1 = x_1(1 + r_s) + x_2(1 + r_F) \tag{36}$$

and

$$Y_2 = x_1(1 + r_s) + x_2\, q \tag{37}$$

where x_1 and x_2 are the proportion of lender's wealth (or capital) committed to the safe and the risky assets respectively and q is the proportion of the original loan repaid; In the case of default q will be $= 0$; in the case of less serious debt problem $q < 1$.

Expected utility, if we assume a constant elasticity utility function for lenders, is given by

$$E(U) = \frac{1}{(1 - C)}\, W^{1-C}[\pi_a Y_1^{1-C} + (1 - \pi_a) Y_2^{1-C}] \tag{38}$$

where π_a is the probability of the good state obtaining, π_b (defined as $\pi_b = [1 - \pi_a]$), the probability of the bad state obtaining, and C the measure of the constant degree of relative risk aversion.

Since we assumed that $x_1 + x_2 = 1$ (and thus that $x_2 = 1 - x_1$) we can rewrite equations (36) and (37) only in terms of x_1 as

$$Y_1 = x_1(r_s - r_F)) + 1 - r_F \tag{39}$$

and

$$Y_2 = x_1(1 + r_s - q) + q \tag{40}$$

Substituting equations (39) and (40) in equation (38) and maximising expected utility with respect to x_1 we get

$$\frac{dE(u)}{dx_1} = 0 \quad \Leftrightarrow \quad \frac{\pi_a}{y_1^c}\,(r_F - r_s) = \frac{1 - \pi_a}{y_2^c}\,(1 + r_s - q)$$

$$\frac{1 - \pi_a}{\pi_a}\;\frac{1 + r_s - q}{r_F - r_s} = \left(\frac{y_2}{y_1}\right)^c$$

$$\frac{1 - \pi_a}{\pi_a}\;\frac{1 + r_s - q}{r_F - r_s} = \left(\frac{x_1\,(1 + r_s - q) + q}{x_1\,(r_s - r_F) + 1 + r_F}\right)^c$$

If we set $Z_1 = r_F - r_s$ and $Z_2 = 1 + r_s - q$ we can derive an explicit solution for x_1, the optimum proportion of the lender's portfolio allocated to the safe asset,

$$X_1 = \frac{\left(\frac{1-\pi_a}{\pi_a}\frac{Z_2}{Z_1}\right)^{1/C}(1+r_F) - q}{Z_2 + Z_1\left(\frac{1-\pi_a}{\pi_a}\frac{Z_2}{Z_1}\right)^{1/C}} \qquad (41)$$

The solution for x_2, the optimum proportion of the lender's portfolio allocated to the risky asset here represented by a sovereign loan, follows.

$$X_2 = 1 - X_1 = \frac{(1+r_s)\left[1-\left(\frac{1-\pi_a}{\pi_a}\frac{Z_2}{Z_1}\right)^{1/C}\right]}{\left(\frac{1-\pi_a}{\pi_a}\frac{Z_2}{Z_1}\right)^{1/C} Z_1 + Z_2} \qquad (42)$$

This allows us to say that the supply of sovereign loans to developing countries given by $W(1 - x_1)$ is an increasing function of q and a decreasing function of the probability of default (or of the bad state obtaining).

Moreover, the optimal amount of lending to the LDCs will decline with a rise in the rate of return on the safe asset, r_s, if C is low; it will grow with a rise in r_F if C is sufficiently low and $(I - \pi_a)$ is independent of r.

NOTES

1. For the proof of this statement see Copeland and Weston (1988, ch.7).
2. The equilibrium proportion of each asset in the market portfolio is given by the market value of individual asset/market value of all assets.
3. Chebyshev's inequality affirms that if y is a random variable with mean m and variance σ^2, then $Pr(|y - m| \geq d) \leq \sigma^2/d^2$ where d is any positive number and $Pr(|y - m) > d)$ is the probability that y will differ from m by at least $\pm d$.
4. For a proof see Fama, E.F. (1971).
5. A Taylor series expansion around $R = 0$ with higher-order terms neglected.
6. For a discussion about the complexity of lending see Walter (1981).

3 The demand for foreign loans

Looking at the demand side of the foreign loans market, the basic question is why a country should borrow and what the optimal level of debt is.

This question is certainly addressed by the growth-cum-debt literature and related models designed to explain the functions of foreign aid in the economic development of a country.

According to these models, external capital is used for capital formation; or, in other words, it is basically seen as a way to expand the resources available for investment. Other models of foreign borrowing, in which the borrowing country's economic policymakers are assumed to be concerned with the optimal allocation of consumption, stress the role of external finance in smoothing the consumption path of a country over time.

Risk aversion and uncertainty also play an important role in determining the demand for foreign loans in models where income is highly variable or sometimes even stochastic. Since borrowing countries are adverse to the variability in (or uncertainty about) their national product, they use foreign capital to compensate for the volatility of income and to permit smooth absorption or consumption.

The following sections give a general idea of the structure of the models designed to determine how much a country should borrow.

3.1 A SCHEMATIC VIEW

In models postulating that countries import capital to finance their economic development, the main purpose of borrowing is to reach and sustain more rapid growth than would otherwise be possible. Borrowing countries may also be interested in smoothing their investment and consumption paths over time.

This smoothing function is implicit, and of secondary importance, in models where the main reason for borrowing is to finance development. But it is the principal objective when high priority is assigned to the optimal allocation of consumption, or in models that posit income variability or uncertainty and the borrowing country's authorities are assumed to be risk-adverse.

For an overview of the categories to which the models we are going to analyse belong the following diagram is helpful:

- MODELS THAT STRESS THE DEVELOPMENT FUNCTION OF FOREIGN CAPITAL
  - GAPS MODELS
  - CYCLE MODELS
- MODELS THAT STRESS THE SMOOTHING FUNCTION OF FOREIGN CAPITAL
  - OPTIMAL ALLOCATION MODELS
  - MODELS WITH INCOME VARIABILITY
  - MODELS WITH INCOME UNCERTAINTY

As we see, the models that stress the development function can be sub-classified into gaps models and cycle models.

According to gaps models, borrowing on the international market is defined as any gap between the investment and savings decisions of a developing country.

Cycle models stress the idea that loan demand depends on the stage of the development cycle of the borrowing country.

3.2 THE CLASSICAL FRAMEWORK OF DEVELOPMENT WITH EXTERNAL FINANCE

First, let us describe the classical theoretical framework developed by Chenery and Strout (1966) for the analysis of the development process given external assistance. In other words, we shall examine the process whereby economic growth can be accelerated thanks to external capital over a limited period of time. The attempt to increase output without recourse to external borrowing may be frustrated by bottlenecks (insufficient savings and investment, lack of human skills, inefficient productive technology and so on).

By relieving these constraints, foreign assistance can make possible fuller use of domestic resources and hence accelerated growth. Here we consider the case in which there are only two resource limits, on skills and on savings, which makes the situation under examination one of investment-limited growth.

The process by which self-sustaining growth can be achieved by using external finance to fill the temporary gap between investment ability and saving's capacity can be derived from the following description of the economic structure. Gross national product, Y_t, equals gross domestic savings, S_t, plus consumption, C_t:

$$Y_t = S_t + C_t \tag{1}$$

Gross domestic savings equal gross investment, I_t, less net inflow of foreign capital, F_t:

$$S_t = I_t - F_t \tag{2}$$

There are three limits to the country's economic growth: a capacity limit based on the Harrod-Domar assumption that a specified amount of investment is needed to increase output; a skill limit following from the idea that the absorptive capacity for additional investment at any time is limited by the supply of complementary inputs, which can only be increased as a result of the development process itself; and a savings limit, which includes not only the marginal propensity to save, but also the government's ability to increase total savings by tax and other measures. These limits can be formally represented by equations (3), (4) and (5):

$$Y_t \leq Y_0 + \frac{1}{K} \sum_{T=0}^{T=t-1} I_t, \qquad K = \frac{I_{t-1}}{Y_t - Y_{t-1}} \tag{3}$$

$$I_t \leq (1 + \delta) I_{t-1} \tag{4}$$

$$S_t \leq S = S_0 + S'(Y_t - Y_0) \tag{5}$$

where K, $K = \frac{I_{t-1}}{Y_t - Y_{t-1}}$, is the incremental gross capital-output ratio;

δ is the maximum rate of growth of investment;

S indicates potential gross domestic savings;

S' represents the marginal rate of savings.

The country aims at a target growth rate represented by a given rate of increase in GNP:

$$Y_t \leq (1 + \bar{g}) Y_{t-1} \tag{6}$$

where g is the target rate of growth for GNP. This corresponds to the generally accepted thesis that developing countries identify the main goal of development as a specified rate of increase of GNP.

In the model outlined above it is assumed that foreign assistance is limited, since the availability of external finance depends on the developing country's future economic prospects, and this puts a constraint on the total amount a country can afford to borrow.

To complete the model we make two further assumptions. We first assume that external borrowing is limited, or expensive, so that the recipient country will use foreign loans mainly for investment purposes to secure some rise in GNP; and secondly we assume that the borrower's objective, provided that the target growth rate is attained, is the maximisation of consumption. Under the assumptions made there is no incentive to build excess capacity or to increase aid by reducing saving.

The increase in GNP will be limited first by the capacity to invest and then by the target growth rate if the investment rate reaches the level required to sustain it.

We distinguish two phases in the development process. Phase 1 is characterised by a constant growth in investment at the annual rate of α and by an accelerating growth of GNP and is described by equations (1) – (5), where equations (3) and (5) are now equalities instead of inequalities.

Solving the system for the level of capital inflow gives:

$$F_t = F_0 + (\delta K - S')(Y_t - Y_0) \tag{7}$$

where $F_0 = I_0 - S_0$.

The increment in external capital, $(F_t - F_0)$, finances the difference between the increment in investment and the increment in savings. External capital fills the gap between investment and savings and the demand for foreign loans is motivated by the developing country's intention of attaining a higher growth rate.

Phase 1 ends in year *m,* when investment reaches a level adequate to sustain the target rate of growth:

$$I_m = K\bar{g}Y_m \tag{8}$$

In the second phase, GNP and investment rise at a constant rate with external assistance determined by the difference between Kg and S_t where

$$S_t = (S_0 - S')\frac{Y_0}{Y_t} + S'$$

In order for the rate of capital inflow to decline the marginal rate of saving S' must exceed the investment rate of Kg required by the growth rate. If this condition is satisfied, the system can be solved for the level of GNP in year p, when the saving rate has risen sufficiently to eliminate the capital inflow:

$$Y_P = \frac{(S' - S_m)}{S' - Kg} Y_m \tag{9}$$

It is important to note that the process of growth with a varying inflow of capital requires continual adjustment of imports and exports to make the trade gap equal the desired gap between investment and saving.

3.3 THE DEVELOPMENT CYCLE THEORY OF INDEBTEDNESS

The development cycle theory of indebtedness (Beenstock, 1983) revives an old idea. This theory too posits that the credit stems from the desire of developing countries to finance their economic development.

Countries tend to be highly leveraged during the early stages of their development, when finance is needed for infrastructure, urbanisation and so on. The demand for foreign loans declines as developing countries reach the more mature phases of their development cycle (see Figure 3.1).

If we want to formalize the idea, even if in general terms, we have to identify an indicator of the stage of economic development and an indicator of the intensity of economic development.

Following Beenstock (1983) we select as an indicator of the stage of economic development the *per capita* GNP (GNP/POP) and as an indicator of the intensity of development the share of investment in GDP (I/GDP).

Figure 3.1
The development cycle theory of indebtedness

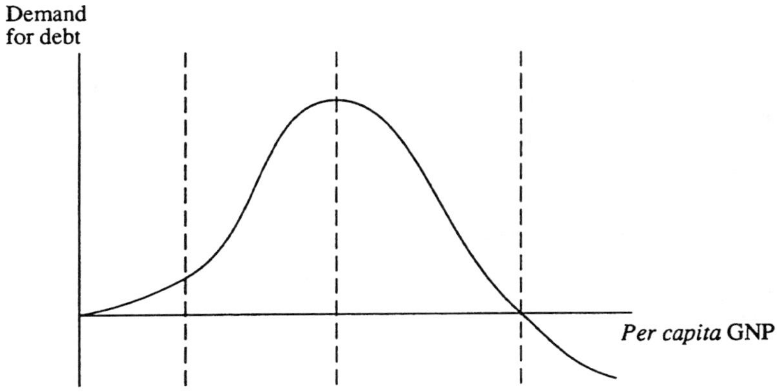

The demand for credit D^d, i.e. the country's foreign debt, will, as a first approximation, take the simple form

$$D^d = f\left(\frac{GNP}{POP}, \frac{I}{GDP}\right) \tag{10}$$

However, if we want the demand for credit to take the profile shown in Figure 3.1, we need to insert a quadratic term in per capita GNP. Moreover, if we want a more sophisticated and complete expression, we would need to introduce as an explanatory variable the interest rate, which represents the cost of borrowing, and normalize debt with respect to GNP since we would expect there to be more debt outstanding in a large country than in a small country.

The demand for external finance will now take the form

$$\frac{D^d}{GNP} = f\left(\frac{GNP}{POP}, \left(\frac{GNP}{POP}\right)^2, \frac{I}{GDP}, r\right). \tag{11}$$

There is a positive relationship between indebtedness and the *per capita* GNP and between indebtedness and the quadratic term in *per capita* GNP. More precisely, as represented in Figure 3.1, in the phase of immaturity, when *per capita* GNP is low, the demand for credit is low too. As GNP begins to rise, in the stage of rapid development, the demand grows very rapidly and peaks. Thereafter development becomes less intense and old debt may be paid off more rapidly than new debt is incurred.

Finally, in the last phase of maturity the demand for credit becomes negative, as the country might wish to become a creditor.

Further we must consider the possibility of a country generating savings itself. In this case, a country's demand for finance is given by

$$D = D^d - S \tag{12}$$

where S designates domestic savings.

If we assume that savings varies directly with the rate of interest r and *per capita* GNP,

$$S = f(GNP/POP, r) \tag{13}$$

we can graphically represent the D^d schedule and the S schedule, for given assumptions about *per capita* GNP, as in Figure 3.2.

Figure 3.2
The demand for credit and the supply of credit

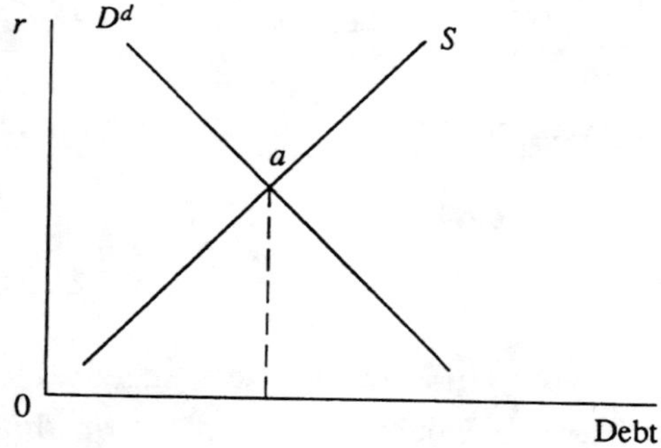

If the country has no access to the international capital market, the entire demand for finance must be satisfied by domestic savings. Equilibrium will be at point a. Gross indebtedness equals OE and is generated entirely through domestic savings. If the country has access to the international capital market we must distinguish two cases: that in which the country is "small" in relation to its risk class and that in which it is "not small". In the first case the debtor country, with its borrowing, does not affect the interest rate applicable to its risk class, and it thus takes the interest rate as given. Equilibrium will move to point *b* in Figure 3.3 and gross indebtedness will be equal to *OM* of which *LM* is owed to international creditors.

Figure 3.3
The equilibrium in the credit market when the country is small in relation to its risk class

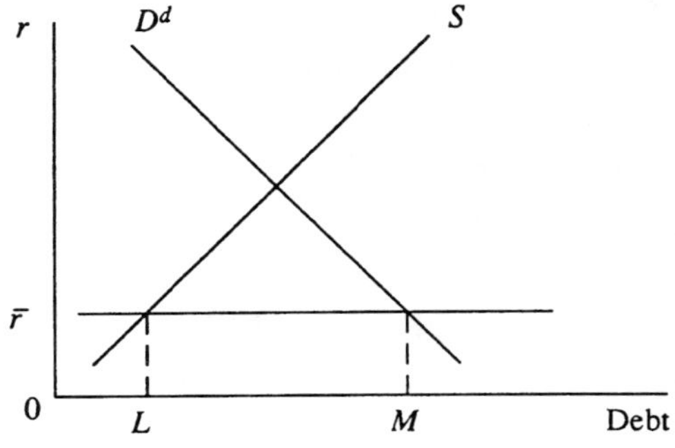

When the borrowing country is "not small" in relation to its risk class, its international borrowing will raise the interest rate charged on foreign loans. We now have to graph a new schedule which represents the supply of finance, D^s, as an increasing function of *r*.

In this case equilibrium will be at point c in Figure 3.4. Gross indebtedness equals *ON* of which *OR* is raised from the international capital market.

Figure 3.4
The equilibrium in the credit market when the country is "not small" in to relation to its risk

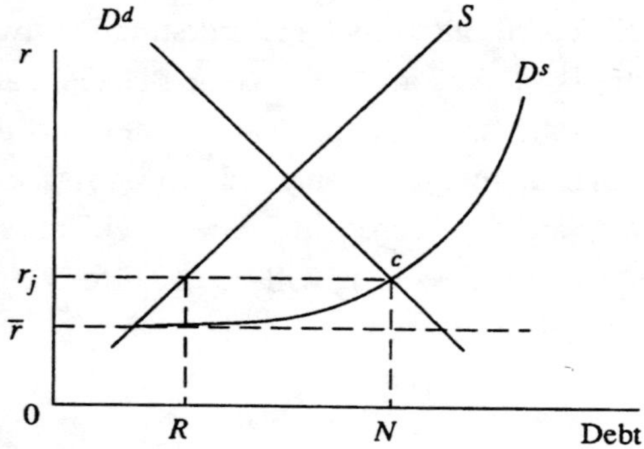

3.4 THE HEFFERNAN MODEL OF THE DEMAND FOR FOREIGN LOANS

A model for the demand for external loans based on a restatement of the development cycle hypothesis is outlined by Heffernan (1983). In this model borrowing countries import capital in the form of sovereign loans to finance economic development. If the country's domestic capital base is insufficient to meet its growth rate target, it will raise capital on the international market. Moreover, according to this restatement of the development cycle hypothesis of indebtedness the demand for external capital is based on expectations of higher future income.

We start from a production function that describes how factor inputs in the borrowing country are used to generate output

$$Y_t = f(N_t, K_t)(1_t \mu_t) \tag{14}$$

In equation (14) Y_t is national product of the borrowing country at time t; N_t and K_t are labour and capital at time t and u_t is a random disturbance term drawn from a stationary, normal distribution.

The inclusions of U_t in the production function means that the national income of the borrowing country may be affected by random shocks. A negative random shock means a bad year; a positive one, a good year.

Loans can be raised on the international capital market at interest rate r. The borrower decides how much capital to raise in the next period, attempting to maximize next period's expected national product or to maximize national welfare defined as a function of GNP.

If the objective is the maximization of expected national product, the problem can be schematized as follows:

$$\max E_{t-1}[P_t Y_t(K_t) - R_t(K_t - DK_t)] \tag{15}$$

where P_t is the price of Y_t, known at $t-1$; R_t is the nominal rental on capital at t, known at $t-1$; DK_t is the domestically owned capital stock.

Under the assumptions made, an incentive for borrowing exists if there is an excess demand for current capital goods and hence if higher future income is expected.

The solution to the borrower's maximization problem and in particular the first order conditions for a maximum give:

$$P_t \frac{\delta Y_t}{\delta K_t} - R_t = 0 \tag{16}$$

If the production function is fully specified, equation (16) can be solved for the optimum level of capital stock, K^*.

The borrowing country's optimum external debt will be given by

$$D^* = K_t^* - DK_t \tag{17}$$

If we assume that the production function is a Cobb-Douglas,

$$Y_t = AK_t^{\alpha} N_t^{\beta} \tag{18}$$

where A is the technical progress parameter, α is the elasticity of output with respect to capital and β is the output elasticity with respect to labour, expected national product becomes

$$E_{t-1}\ [P_t A K_t^{\alpha} N_t^{\beta} - R_t (K_t - DK_t)] \tag{19}$$

and the solution to the borrower's maximization problem gives

$$K_t^* = \frac{P_t Y_t \alpha}{R_t} \tag{20}$$

and

$$D^* = \frac{P_t Y_t \alpha}{R_t} - DK_t \tag{21}$$

The demand for external capital is negatively correlated with the world rental rate on capital, R_t (which in turn is a positive function of the world interest rate) and with the domestic supply of capital, which represents the fruit of cumulated past savings. The demand for external capital varies positively with the national product, Y_t, and with its price, P_t.

Alternatively it can be assumed that the country wishes to maximize national welfare where the utility or welfare of the country depends on the level of national income.

Since income is subject to random shocks, at the beginning of each year the outcome at the end of the year is unknown and the existence of uncertainty means that the borrower is really maximizing an expected utility function. If the borrower is indifferent to risk, the country welfare is a linear function of its national income. But if it is adverse to risk, the relationship between its welfare and national income will be curved and more precisely the curve will be concave from below. The specification of a nation's social welfare function on the demand side allows one to take account of political factors, which are seen by risk analysts as exerting significant influence on the decisions to borrow in the international capital markets.

3.5 BORROWING AS A MEANS TO SMOOTH CONSUMPTION OVER TIME

Economic policymakers in the borrowing country, of course, may not be concerned primarily with the growth of GNP; they can be interested in careful calculation of intertemporal consumption possibilities. As we have seen, the traditional growth-cum-debt literature focuses on the investment motive for using external finance. When policymakers are interested in the intertemporal allocation of consumption, on the other hand, external finance is demanded and used to smooth the consumption path over time (Cooper-Sachs, 1986).

The optimal borrowing problem thus becomes:

$$\text{Max } V = \sum_{i=0}^{T} (1 + \rho)^{-i} U(C_i) \tag{22}$$

subject to

$$K_{t+1} = K_t(1 - d) + It \tag{23}$$

$$Y_t = F(K_t) \tag{24}$$

$$D_{t+1} = (1 + r) D_t + (I_t + C_t) - Y_t \tag{25}$$

$$\lim (1 + r)^{-t} D_t = O \tag{26}$$

$$K_0, D_0 \text{ given} \tag{27}$$

C_i is real consumption in period i, $U(C_i)$ is instantaneous utility in period i ($U' > O$ and $U'' < 0$), and V represents intertemporal utility given by a discounted sum of instantaneous utilities where ρ measures the rate of subjective time discount. Output at time t is a function of current capital stock, K_t, and it is implicit that labour is held fixed at $L_t = 1$.

K_t evolves according to the path of investment, and in equation (23) d is the rate of depreciation and I_t is gross capital formation.

D_{t+1} is the stock of foreign debt at the end of period t which equals the debt outstanding at the start of period $t + 1$, $[(1 + r)D_t]$, minus the trade balance during the period t, $TB_t = Y_t - I_t - C_t$; r represents the interest rate paid on foreign debt.

Forming the Lagrangian we get

$$L = \sum_{0}^{\infty}(1+\rho)^{-t}\{U(C_t) + \mu_t[D_{t+1} - D_t(1+r) - I_t - C_t + Y_t(K_t)] +$$
$$\lambda_t[K_{t+1} - K_t(1-d) - I_t]\} \tag{28}$$

First order conditions give

$$\frac{dL}{dC_t} = 0 \Rightarrow U_c = \mu_t \tag{29}$$

$$\frac{dL}{dD_t} = 0 \Rightarrow (1 + r)\,\mu_t = (1 + \rho)\,\mu_{t-1} \tag{30}$$

$$\frac{dL}{dI_t} = 0 \Rightarrow \lambda_t = -\mu_t$$

$$\frac{dL}{dK_t} = 0 \Rightarrow \lambda_t\,(1-d) = \mu_t Y_{kt} \tag{31}$$

μ_t is the dynamic Lagrange multiplier attached to D_t and it represents the marginal utility of wealth; λ_t is the shadow value of capital;

$$U_c = \frac{dU(C_t)}{dC_t} \quad \text{and} \quad Y_{kt} = \frac{dY\,(K_t)}{d_{kt}}$$

The system we get is a four dimensional, non-linear differential equation system in λ_t, μ_t, k_t and D_t and can be solved fully specifying the utility function and the production function and assuming particular values for the relevant parameters.

The results of the optimising behaviour in terms of consumption are straightforward. With a perfect world capital market, borrowing should be undertaken to smooth the marginal utility of consumption over time. The marginal utility of consumption in period t is

$$(MUC_t) = \frac{dU(C_t)}{dC_t} \,/\, (1 + \rho)^t \tag{32}$$

The present value price of output in period t is

$$\pi_t = (1 + r)^{-t} \tag{33}$$

where π_t represents the number of units of output that must be saved at time 0 in order to yield one unit of goods in period t. The consumption smoothing rate is then

$$\frac{MUC_t}{\pi_t} = \mu \qquad \text{for all periods of } t \text{ where } \mu \text{ is the} \tag{34}$$

marginal utility of wealth.

3.6 THE IMPLICIT COST OF EXTERNAL FINANCE

There is a literature that challenges the conventional view of the benefits of external finance, citing the negative correlation between domestic savings and external finance found in a number of empirical studies (Grinols and Bhagwati (1976;1979); Bhagwati (1978); Wasow (1979)).

What these analyses actually show is a reduction in the domestic savings rate associated with resort to external finance.

This negative relationship may be easily explained and understood if we do not view external finance only as a means for accelerating growth but also, as just noted, as a way of achieving more efficient intertemporal allocation of consumption.

Consider, for example, an increase in the inflow of foreign capital. If all the additional aid is invested, it generates higher potential consumption in the future, but present consumption remains unchanged. Some of this enhanced future consumption may be brought forward in time, thereby reducing current domestic savings.

Rational response to real economic shocks may also give rise to a negative relationship between savings and capital inflow. Take as an example an economy subject to variability of export revenues. If the possibility of external financial transactions is non-existent, then the burden of export shortfalls will be borne by current consumption, whereas external financial transactions could be used to shift consumption from years in which export performance is above trend to years when it is below.

However, models designed to deal with the intertemporal optimization of external finance are not consistent with the static, one-period framework of the present work.

3.7 INCOME VARIABILITY AND THE DEMAND FOR FOREIGN LOANS

A model that takes income variability into account in a more explicit way than Heffernan is that developed by Eaton and Gersovitz. In "Debt with potential repudiation: theoretical and empirical analysis", they stress the fact that countries generally experience periods of high and low income relative to trend, and they argue that this variance in their income can play a crucial role in determining the amount they want to borrow and, more germane to our present purposes, also the amount they can be safely lent.

The model posits that a country borrows in bad periods, when income is below trend, contracting the obligation to repay in good times when income is high. Failure to repay prevents borrowing in subsequent periods. Trend income and consumption growth are assumed the same. The borrower may also lend in international capital markets in high-income periods and liquidate investments in poor periods, a process we refer to as savings. We indicate with y the initial level of trend income; g is the growth rate of trend and σ the percentage by which income deviates from trend. The country borrows a percent $b>0$ of σ and saves a percent $s > 0$ of σ at gross rates of interest r and r' respectively.

The borrower consumes c^1 in a low-income period where

$$c^1(s,b,t,) = [1 - \sigma\,(1 - b - \frac{r's}{G})]yG^t \qquad (35)$$

$$t = 0, 2, 4$$

and c^h in a high-income period where

$$c^h(s,b,t,) = [1 + \sigma\,(1 - \frac{rb}{G} - s)]\,yG^t \qquad (36)$$

$$t = 1, 3, 5$$

The utility of consumption in each period is given by a constant relative risk-aversion utility function:

$$U(C) = \frac{C^{1-\gamma}}{1-\gamma}$$

where γ is the measure of relative risk aversion.

The utility of consumption t periods in the future is discounted by ρ_t where $0<\rho<1$.

Moreover we define the two discounted utilities W^h and W^1 according to whether the perspective is from a high-income or low-income period as

$$W_t^h\ (s,b) = U[C^h\ (s,b,t)] + \rho U[C^1(s,b,t+1)] \tag{37}$$

$$W_t^1\ (s,b) = U[C^1\ (s,b,t)] + \rho U[C^h(s,b,t+1)] \tag{38}$$

When $C = C^h$ the borrower maximizes W^h with respect to s, given b.

When $C = C^1$ the borrower maximizes W^1 with respect to b, given s.

This rule determines optimal values of s and b on the assumption of repayment. In deriving first order conditions, first we substitute (35) and (36) into (37) and (38) and for convenience we assume $y = 1$. This yields:

$$\frac{\delta w_t^h}{\delta s\ |b} = [1-\sigma\,(1-b-\frac{r's}{G}]^{-\gamma} \quad - \frac{G^\gamma}{\rho r'}[1+\sigma\,(1-\frac{rb}{G}-s)]^{-\gamma}=0 \tag{39}$$

$$\frac{\delta w_t^1}{\delta b\ |s} = [1-\sigma\,(1-b-\frac{r's}{G}]^{-\gamma} \ -G^{-\gamma}\rho r\,[1+\sigma\,(1-\frac{rb}{G}-s)]^{-\gamma}=0 \tag{40}$$

From this it can be argued that an unconstrained borrower will typically choose to smooth absorption by specialising in either lending or borrowing. In fact, looking at first order conditions, we observe that if

$$G^\gamma > \rho\ (r'r)^{1/2} \tag{41}$$

desired borrowing is positive while desired savings is zero. Conversely if

$$G^\gamma < \rho\ (r'r)^{1/2} \tag{42}$$

desired borrowing is zero while desired savings is positive. And finally if

$$G^\gamma = \rho\ (r'r)^{1/2} \tag{41}$$

the borrower is indifferent between smoothing via borrowing and via lending.

In other words, an equilibrium with positive borrowing will be found only when the growth rate is large relative to the discount factor and to the geometric average of the borrowing and lending rates.

If $g^{\gamma} > \rho(rr')^{1/2}$ the desired amount of borrowing relative to income will be

$$\sigma b^* = \frac{\sigma[1 + (\rho r)^{-1/\gamma} G] + [(\rho r)^{-1/\gamma} G - 1]}{[1 + (\rho r)^{-1/\gamma} r]} \tag{42}$$

This means that desired borrowing (or the demand for foreign loans) depends positively on the growth rate G and the standard deviation of income σ.

Now let us introduce uncertainty about the borrower's situation in the period in which loans come due. In this case, we assume further that there is no growth ($G = 1$) and no saving $r' = 0$.

We now assume that the borrower's income in any future period takes on values $y^l = 1 - \sigma$ and $y^h = 1 + \sigma$ with equal probability regardless of income in the previous period. Borrowing occurs in period t if and only if $y^t = y^l$, $b_{t-1} = 0$ and the borrower has not previously defaulted.

Loans are due in any period regardless of income in that period. Lenders are risk-neutral and in competition among themselves. Borrowers may borrow at the safe interest rate r only if they are willing to repay in the following period regardless of the actual value of income in that period. Given that they will repay, unconstrained borrowers will select b to maximize utility given by

$$U[1 - \sigma(1 - b) + \rho[U[1 + \sigma(1 - rb)] + U[1 - \sigma(1 + rb]\}/2 \tag{43}$$

Approximating this expression by a second-order Taylor series expression[1] about $c = 1$ gives as an expression for optimal borrowing

$$\sigma b^* = \frac{(1-\rho r)/V + \sigma}{(1+\rho r^2)} \tag{44}$$

where $V = U''/U'$ is the degree of absolute risk aversion. Again there is a positive relationship between optimal borrowing and the standard deviation of income.

3.8 BORROWING AS A MEANS OF REDUCING INCOME UNCERTAINTY

We next apply the theoretical framework of a model of insurance and saving developed by Hey and Fiocca (1983) to the case of a developing country demanding loans on the international capital market. The economic agent is the borrowing country, and it is pictured as existing in a finite-horizon world with discrete periods. In each period the country has an income which is ex-ante uncertain and in each period it must decide how much to borrow. Its utility function depends only on income and is assumed to be additively separable. Risk aversion is also assumed, so that the utility function is taken to be concave in that period's income.

Being risk-averse, the borrowing country dislikes the income uncertainty and would like to eliminate it. By entering into a contract with a lender country (call it an insurance contract or a borrowing contract) the borrowing country may succeed in reducing the "riskiness" related to future income.

Under the contract a cost equal to C is borne by the borrowing country to reduce the standard deviation of its income from σ to $\sigma - T$.

The lender wishes to enter into such a contract up to the point of indifference between entering and not entering. With the contract the distribution of the borrowing country's income changes from $N(\mu, \sigma^2)$ to $N\{\mu - C(\sigma - T)^2\}$, where C is the cost of reducing the standard deviation, T is the reduction in the standard deviation and C and T are related in some fashion.

Figure 3.5a
The distribution of the borrowing country's income before entering the contract with the lender country

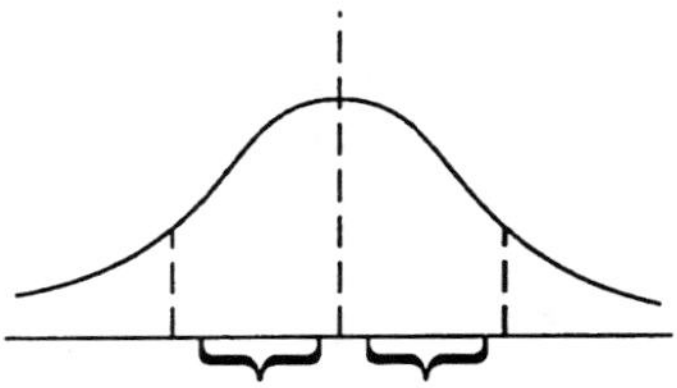

Figure 3.5b
The distribution of the borrowing country's income after entering the contract with the lender country

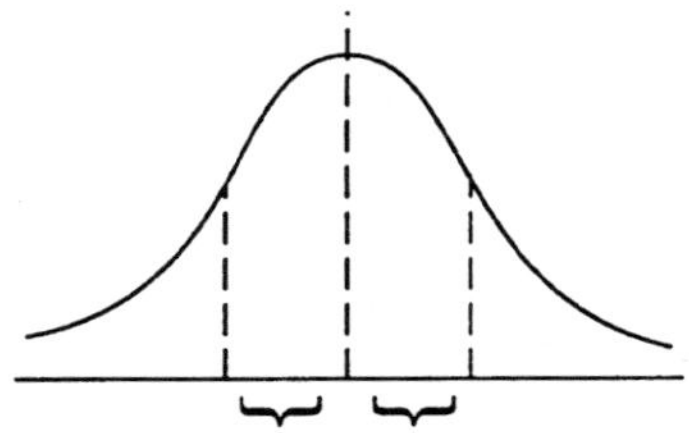

In other words, we are speaking about an arrangement that closely resembles an unfair insurance contract which allows the agent to reduce the standard deviation of income while keeping the mean constant at a cost related to the extent of the reduction in the standard deviation. As mentioned, our initial random variable is y. We now suppose that the contract transforms the realized y into x.

The lender country's income, z, is thus given by

$$z = C + (y - x) \tag{45}$$

If we assume that the lender's utility depends on its income and that he displays constant absolute risk aversion, it is possible to demonstrate (Hey and Fiocca, 1989) that the relationship between C and T is one of proportionality.

$$C = \theta T \tag{46}$$

where θ is the proportionality factor.

The distribution of ex-ante income changes with the borrowing contract from:

$$N(\mu, \sigma^2) \quad \text{to} \quad N\{\mu - \theta T^2, (\sigma - T)^2\}$$

Consider, now, a one-period world. The borrowing country's utility function depends on income, y.

$$U = U(y) \tag{47}$$

Moreover we take the utility function to be constant absolute risk averse:

$$U(y) = -e^{(-Vy)} \tag{48}$$

where V represents the degree of absolute risk aversion.

Since income is uncertain, the borrowing country maximises expected utility as given by

$$E(U) = -e^{-V(\mu - \theta T^2) + 1/2V^2(\sigma - T)^2} \tag{49}$$

In other words, the borrowing country selects the amount of the reduction in the standard deviation of income so as to maximise equation (51).

The solution to the maximisation problem gives

$$T^* = V\sigma / -(2\theta + V \tag{50}$$

Considering T as a proxy for the amount a country wishes to borrow, it follows that the demand for foreign loans depends positively on the country's standard deviation of income, σ, and on the degree of absolute risk aversion, V. It depends negatively on θ, which represents the proportionality factor between the cost of "borrowing" and the amount the country would like to borrow.

NOTES

1. Because introducing stochastic income makes it impossible to derive exact analytic expressions from the constant relative risk-aversion utility function.

4 Why debt problems might arise from the borrower's perspective

Foreign loans are a particular contractual arrangement between suppliers of capital and users of capital. The borrower promises to pay the lender certain amounts at certain times, but in some circumstances he may not be able or may not wish to meet these obligations.

At this point, one crucial difference between domestic and foreign loans comes into play. Domestic debts are legally enforceable claims, whereas, foreign loans are covered by no legal institution to ensure that the borrower actually discharges his obligation.

In the literature two basic conceptual approaches to the occurrence of debt problems are found, which we may label the ability-to-pay and the willingness- to-pay approaches. To these approaches correspond three possible explanations of why repayment problems may arise. A borrower country may not discharge its debt service because it cannot pay (i.e. is insolvent), because it is illiquid, or just because it elects not to pay. The first two explanations coincide with the ability-to-pay approach, the third to the willingness-to-pay approach.

- **Ability to pay** { **Cannot pay/insolvency** / **Illiquidity**
- **Willingness to pay** → **Elects not to pay**

4.1 THE ABILITY-TO-PAY APPROACH

The ability-to-pay approach posits fundamentally that a country gets into debt problems for technical financial motives and hence fails to make the payments due for reasons beyond its control. As to insolvency, to understand what is relevant in evaluating the ability of the borrower to repay a loan we need to consider two identities.

The first is the balance-of-trade identity, which says that if D is total debt; ΔD, ($\Delta D = D_{t-1} - D_t$), repayment of the debt, r the interest rate and TB the trade balance (or resource balance), in each period the following holds:

$$D_{t-1} - D_t = TB_t + rD_t \qquad (1)$$

The second relevant identity is the finance identity

$$D_{t-1} - D_t = (S_t - I_t) + (T_t - G_t) \qquad (2)$$

where S is private savings, I domestic investment, T tax revenue and G government spending. According to the finance identity, in each period repayment of debt equals the sum of private and government savings. Thus, generally speaking, a country's ability to service its debt is related both to the trade surplus and to private and government savings.

Under the insolvency variant of the cannot-pay approach, there are three possible interpretations of why debt problems may occur. All three treat the resources available for repayment as an exogenous variable.

The first interpretation says that debt problems arise when the present value of the debtor nation's available resources falls short of the present value of debt service, so that the intertemporal budget constraint is not satisfied. In terms of equation (1) consider the case in which domestic product is independent of T and the government is unconstrained and can set $T = Y$ and $G = I = O$. It follows that $S_t = rD_{t-1}$ and we can write

$$D_{t-1} - D_t = Y_t - rD_{t-1} \qquad (3)$$

From (3) we readily derive

$$D_0 - \frac{D_t}{(1+r)^t} = \frac{Y_1}{(1+r)} + \ldots + \frac{Y_t}{(1+r)^t} \tag{4}$$

and hence the condition for a country to be solvent is

$$D_0 = \frac{Y_1}{(1+r)} + \ldots + \frac{Y_t}{(1+r)^t} \tag{5}$$

or looking at the transversality condition,

$$\lim_{t \to \infty} \frac{Y_t}{(1+r)^t} \to 0 \tag{6}$$

In other words, for a country to be able to repay its debt, the intertemporal budget constraint must be satisfied and this is so if the discounted sum of the debtor's resources, here proxied by the income streams, adds up to the initial face value of debt.

Moreover, we can say that condition (5) is satisfied if and only if, at the limit, the discounted value of debt tends to zero (transversality condition).

The second variant of the cannot-pay explanation centres on the present discounted value of the balance-of-trade or resource balance. Now, instead of looking at equation (4) we should look at

$$D_0 - \frac{D_t}{(1+r)^t} = \frac{TB_1}{(1+r)} + \ldots + \frac{TB_t}{(1+r)^t} \tag{7}$$

and the condition of solvency becomes

$$D_0 = \frac{TB_1}{(1+r)} + \ldots + \frac{TB_t}{(1+r)^t} \tag{8}$$

In other words the discounted sum of all trade balances must at least equal the initial face value of the debt.

This case differs from the intertemporal budget constraint to the extent that the full present value of income cannot be made available to foreigners, perhaps because there are more tradables.

The last variant of the cannot-pay explanation is based on the idea that as sovereign loans are claims on governments, repayment can be said to depend more on the government's ability to raise revenues than on the net worth of the country.

If a government can impose lump-sum taxation at no cost, then national wealth and maximal government revenue coincide (we are back to the case of equation (4) where we set $Y = T$). But, since taxes usually impose excess burdens and are costly to raise, the maximum amount that a government can extract from an economy is smaller than the net worth of the economy itself.

If this is the case, indicating with τ the constant tax rate that the borrower's government levies on national wealth, the relevant constraint now becomes

$$D_0 - \frac{D_t}{(1+r)^t} = \frac{\tau Y_1}{(1+r)} + \ldots + \frac{\tau Y_t}{(1+r)^t} \qquad (9)$$

and the condition for a country to be able to repay his debt

$$D_0 = \frac{\tau Y_1}{(1+r)} + \ldots + \frac{\tau Y_t}{(1+r)^t} \qquad (10)$$

Debt repayment thus depends on taxing authority as well as on national wealth.

According to country risk analysts,[1] present levels of indebtedness, however, do not appear so high as to exceed the cannot-pay thresholds when calculated on the basis of present value. Consequently, the cannot-pay/solvency approach makes little sense in the current situation.

Let us now look at the liquidity variant. Debt repayment problems may be linked not to insolvency but to the illiquidity of the borrowing country.

A borrower is said to be illiquid when even if he has a positive net worth, he cannot convert the required portion of his net worth into a means of payment. The borrowing country's *current* income, for example, may be inadequate to meet *current* debt service. This may be a transitory problem, however, and if it is viewed as such by lenders they may still be willing to provide additional loans to tide the borrowing country over its temporary illiquidity.

On the other hand, banks may be incapable of the coordination necessary to overcome a liquidity problem.[2]

The importance of coordination among banks depends on the cost of lending. If the cost of lending is constant with respect to the amount lent, such coordination is not relevant to the solution of the illiquidity problem. If, on the other hand, each bank faces an increasing cost of lending, a loan from a single bank will be more expensive than the same size loan from many banks. Thus, it may well be that a single bank cannot protect its loan by extending additional financing until the borrower has overcome the liquidity crisis, but that all banks acting together may find it in their interest to do so.

Moreover, if creditors are not closely coordinated this basically forced lending provides an incentive to individual creditors to act as free riders, relying on others to lend enough to avert default. But we should remember that the debtor country may insist on the prorated participation of each of its creditors in the bailout loan, which at least partially responds to free-rider problem. Thus whether or not a liquidity crisis will turn into insolvency depends essentially on the behaviour of lenders.

Next, we shall examine the situation in which a country, though able to service its debt, chooses not to do so.

4.2 THE WILLINGNESS-TO-PAY APPROACH

It is more and more commonly held by economists that a crucial role in determining debt problems is played by the borrowing country's willingness to pay.

Willingness to pay is particularly important in international loans to sovereign governments because as noted before there is no enforcement machinery to ensure that a sovereign borrower, able to service its debt, will choose to do so.

Once loans have been made, the debtor country has the option to renege on the promise of servicing the debt.

The decision to renege will depend on the costs and benefits associated with it. The nature and the extent of the sanctions that creditors can use to increase the cost of breaking loan contracts are thus critical in determining the behaviour of the borrowing country.

However, when loans are made lenders are aware of the possibility of partial or total default and borrowers are aware of the fact that sanctions might be imposed.

Since the repayment of international debt is largely voluntary, the penalties that may be imposed on a country are at best indirect, even if legislation in some lender countries potentially provides for penalties.[3] Among the principal sanctions are a credit cut-off and various forms of interference with the debtor's international transactions and transfers.

As to a credit cut-off, i.e. an embargo on future borrowing, there are situations in which such a penalty is not operative. For example, in models with a finite time horizon we know, and lenders know, that no loans would be repaid in the last period since there would be no future exclusion to worry about. Consequently, lenders would never make a loan coming due in the last period. But then it is possible to apply the same line of reasoning to the next-to-last period, and so on ad infinitum. Even in an infinite horizon framework, however, a penalty consisting solely of a credit embargo may be ineffective. This would be so, for instance, when there is a point in time beyond which the flow will always be from debtor to creditor. The reasoning that applies is the same as the above.

But if in the future there is always the possibility of flows in both directions (from debtor to creditor and from creditor to debtor), then an embargo on future lending may prove to be an effective sanction. For example, if the income of the borrowing country is volatile and the country is risk-adverse, it will use foreign capital to smooth consumption. In this case the cost of a credit cut-off is the necessity it imposes of finding other methods for consumption smoothing if it is to avoid sharp drops in consumption. Therefore uncertainty is a relevant factor in the effectiveness of a credit ban as a penalty.

Bulow and Rogoff (1986) suggest that a debtor country may divert debt-service payments to accumulate assets that may subsequently be used and replenished to smooth consumption. At some point in time, of course, the borrowing country has to make a decision on whether it is convenient to make a large payment in order to preserve access to the credit market or to acquire an asset that would provide a large and growing amount of insurance against a temporary fall in income. Since the self-insurance option may be a convenient one it follows that a loss of access to credit markets may not be an effective penalty.

Borrowing countries also use foreign loans to finance their international trade, so lenders may use their power to affect transactions as a possible sanction. If this sanction is anticipated, however, the borrower may again choose to accumulate foreign reserves to finance post-default trade instead of using income to repay its debt.[4]

The foregoing makes it clear that accurately modelling penalties and assessing their implications for the debtor is one of the most important problems in the theory of country risk. For now, in any event, let us examine a few relevant models aimed at explaining how borrowers make their decisions about repayment of debt under different circumstances.

4.3 A SIMPLE MODEL WITH PENALTIES FOR ANALYSING BORROWING COUNTRIES' WILLINGNESS TO PAY

The comparative evaluation of alternatives is at the heart of the willingness-to-pay approach. The borrowing country assesses the cost and benefits of defaulting, and if the latter outweighs the former, so that the utility of default is bigger than that of repayment, it will elect not to repay its foreign debt.

We now start analysing the simple model with exogenous penalties developed by Eaton-Gersovitz-Stiglitz (1986).

The basic simplifying assumptions of this model are that the extent and severity of the potential penalties are exogenous and that they do not depend on the characteristics of debtors or creditors. We are in a two-period framework. A loan of amount F is made in the first period with an obligation to repay in the second period $r(F)$, where r is the interest to be paid on the loan.

If the borrower fails to honour the obligation, a fixed penalty P will be imposed. The utility of the borrowing country depends positively on the amount borrowed, $\delta U/\delta F > 0$, and negatively on x, the obligation imposed by the loan agreement ($\delta U/\delta x > 0$) defined as

$x = r(F)$ in the case of repayment
$x = \bar{P}$ in the case of default

In the case of regular repayment, the total utility of the borrower in the second period is given by

$$U_R = U(F, r(F)) \tag{11}$$

In the case of default, the total utility is given by

$$U_d = U(\mathrm{F}, r(\bar{P})) \tag{12}$$

The borrower chooses to repay if

$$U_d \leq U_R \tag{13}$$

If lenders are competitive and face an opportunity cost of funds of i, we have

$$r(F) = (1 + i)F \tag{14}$$

In this case, regular repayment occurs if and only if

$$F \leq \frac{\bar{P}}{(1 + i)} \tag{15}$$

It is now possible to modify the model to take account of uncertainty (Eaton, Gersovitz and Stiglitz, 1986). Introducing uncertainty means that the penalty now depends on the state of nature (S) so instead of having $P = \bar{P}$ we now have

$$P = P(S) \tag{16}$$

The remaining assumptions still hold. The utility of the borrower if he defaults is now

$$U_D = U[L, P, s] \tag{17}$$

Utility of the borrower if he does not default is

$$U_R = U[F, r(F), S] \tag{18}$$

where the appearance of the variable S in the utility function indicates that utility may depend on S in other ways than through P.

The amount of repayment $r(F)$, however, does not depend on s.

The borrowing country repays its debt in all states of nature $s \in S$ for which

$$U_R \geq U_D \tag{19}$$

The borrowing country does not repay its debt, on the other hand, in all states $s \in S'$ for which

$$U_R < U_D \tag{20}$$

Notice that we now speak in terms of expected utility.

The borrower's expected utility is given by

$$\int_{s} U_R f(s) ds \ + \ \int_{s^1} U_D f(s) ds \tag{21}$$

where with $f(s)$ we indicate the probability of state s obtaining.

If lenders are competitive , risk-neutral and facing a constant cost of funds i, then

$$\pi r\,(F) = (1 + i)\,F \tag{22}$$

where π is the probability of repayment given by

$$\pi = \int_S f(s)ds \qquad (23)$$

The model, now incorporating uncertainty, may take account of the fact that payment may not be made and the penalty may be imposed. However, the choice of the borrowing country, or its willingness to pay, still depends on the weighing of alternatives, and more specifically on the comparison between the costs and the benefits associated with a default decision. It is worth noting that while the simple models described consider only the possibility of a complete default, they may be readily modified, as we shall see, to take account of the possibility of partial defaults or reschedulings.

4.4 BORROWING COUNTRIES' WILLINGNESS TO PAY AND THE ENDOGENIETY OF PENALTIES

We now want to consider two cases of endogeniety of the default penalty. The first case refers to a default penalty proportionate to the income of the borrowing country (Cohen, 1989). The second case refers to a default penalty related to the intensity of default undertaken by the borrowing country (Aizenman, 1986). Let us first analyse the possibility of repudiating external debt when the penalty that creditors would impose on the borrowing country consists of a loss proportionate to the borrowing country's income.

We are always in a two-period framework. In the economy there are three different types of agents: households, firms and the government. For what concerns production, the assumptions are that the production functions are identical across firms and that in period 1 the level of installed capital is identical across firms.[5]

Indicating with f_j the production function of firm j, with K_{ij} the initial endowment of capital in period i and with I_{ij} the investment a firm j decide to undertake in period i, in period 2 firm j produces

$$q_{2j} = f_j(K_{1j} + I_{1j}) \qquad (24)$$

The investment program is chosen so as to maximise

$$W_J = \text{Max}\,[f_j(K_{ij}) - I_1 + \frac{1}{1+r} f_j(K_{1j} + I_1)] \tag{25}$$

First order conditions give

$$f_j'[K_{1j} + I_{1j}] = 1 + r \tag{26}$$

For what concern consumption, each consumer wants to maximise utility given by

$$U_i = U_i(C_{1j}) + \rho U_i(C_{2i}) \tag{27}$$

under the constraint

$$C_1 i + \frac{1}{(1+r)} C_{2i} \leq W_i \tag{28}$$

where W_i is agent's i initial wealth and ρ the time discount factor.
First order conditions give

$$u'_1(C_{1i}) = \rho(1+r)\, u'_1(C_{2i}) \tag{29}$$

We can now rewrite the first order conditions for the maximisation of consumers' utility in terms of aggregate consumption as

$$C_1 + \frac{1}{(1+r)} C_2 \leq W \tag{30}$$

where $C_1 = \sum C_{1i}$; $C_2 = \sum C_{2i}$; $W = \sum W_i$

For what concerns the government, we assume that it seeks to maximise social welfare as given by

$$U = \sum \vartheta_i u_i (C_{i1}, C_{i2}) \tag{31}$$

Where $\vartheta_i = W_i/W$ is the fraction of total wealth held by agent i.

If the government acts on behalf of its citizens it will not impose them to repay its foreign debt if no penalties would be imposed by creditors.[6]

Next assumption is, thus, that in case of default lenders will impose on the borrowing country a penalty consisting in reducing the firms' production[7] by

$$f_{di}(K_i) = (1 - \lambda) f_i(K_i) \tag{32}$$

It is important to stress that the effective cost

$$\lambda f = \lambda \sum_i f_i$$

is not captured by lenders and that external debt is a public good since any default undertaken by a national borrower would result in a cost for all national producers.

Let D_i be the debt of each agent and $D_i(1 + r)$ the repayment failing due in period 2. The national authorities will permit private agents to default if the cost of doing so is smaller than the burden of honouring it, or if

$$\lambda \sum f_i(K_i) < \sum D_i(1 + r) \tag{33}$$

Now there are two possibilities for the government: to centralise the debt or to not authorise the debt. If the government centralise the debt, condition (33) holds. If the government does not centralise the debt, lenders may avoid defaults by imposing that each firm's repayment satisfies the following condition:

$$D_i \leq f_i(K_i) \tag{34}$$

Such a rule, however, does not seem very efficient from the borrowing country's point of view since some firms with very high productivity might wish to borrow more than according to equation (34) while others would wish to borrow less and yet the country as a whole will satisfy condition (33).

This inefficiency may be overcome by government intervention. For instance as suggested by Cohen (1989), "the government may itself borrow on foreign markets and redistribute the product of its borrowing to national agents. How would this redistribution take place? One traditional way would be to impose an optimal tax on borrowing so as to spread the macroeconomic constraint, given by (33), efficiently".[8]

Aizenman (1986), instead, makes default penalties contingent upon the intensity of default.

A stochastic fixed penalty may be represented by

$$P = P_0 / \psi$$

where ψ represents a stochastic disturbance whose distribution is assumed to be known to both the lender and the borrower. A penalty contingent upon the intensity of default, on the other hand, may be expressed as

$$P = \tau^h P \qquad h \leq 1 \tag{35}$$

$$= \tau^h P_0 / \psi \qquad 0 \leq \tau \leq 1$$

where τ denotes the default rate and h is the elasticity of the penalty with respect to the default intensity. A higher h implies higher responsiveness of the penalty to the default intensity. Moreover the effective penalty never exceeds P and it approaches P as $\tau \Rightarrow 1$. Varying h will allow an assessment of the role of endogenous penalties, where $h \Rightarrow 1$ will bring convergence to the benchmark case of a fixed penalty.

Again, consider a two-period framework. Borrowing (D) takes place in period 1 at an interest rate r^*, exogenously fixed since the borrowing country is assumed to be a small country. Debt repayment, ($D(1 + r^*)$), is scheduled in period 2. In case of default a penalty P is inflicted upon the borrower. The first problem to be solved is now how the borrowing country chooses the default rate. It is assumed that in period 2 the borrowing country chooses the default rate τ so as to maximise the gain in net income attributed to default. The default income $y(\tau)$ is defined as

$$y(\tau) = \tau D(1 + r^*) - \tau^h P_0 / \psi \qquad (37)$$

where the term $\tau D(1 + r^*)$ represents the benefit of partial default and the term $\tau^h N_0 / \psi$ is the cost associated with the default.

Let us denote with τ the default rate that maximises the default income. Direct optimisation, for $h \geq 1$, gives

$$\tau = \text{Min}\,\{1;[D(1 + r^*)/(hP)]^{1/(h-1)}\} \qquad (38)$$

Graphically, indicating on the vertical axes the marginal cost and marginal benefit associated with the default and on the horizontal axes the default rate, it is easy to show how the optimal default rate is determined.

Figure 4.1
The detemination of the optimal default rate

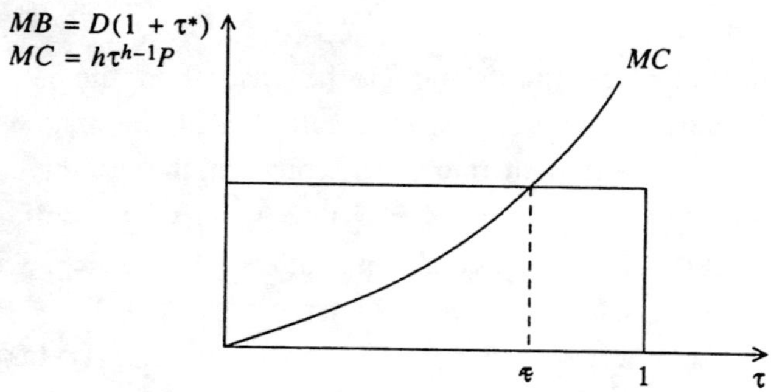

However, it is also possible to show algebrically (Aizenman, 1986 appendix B) that for an internal solution ($0 < \tau < 1$) a rise in the elasticity of the penalty with respect to the default intensity (h) will increase the default rate. Again it is easy to see this result graphically. A rise in h is associated with a rightward shift of the *MC* curve thus causing a rise in the optimal default rate. The same result occurs if we have a drop in the default penalty.

Figure 4.2
The effect on marginal cost of default of a rise in h and a drop in P_0

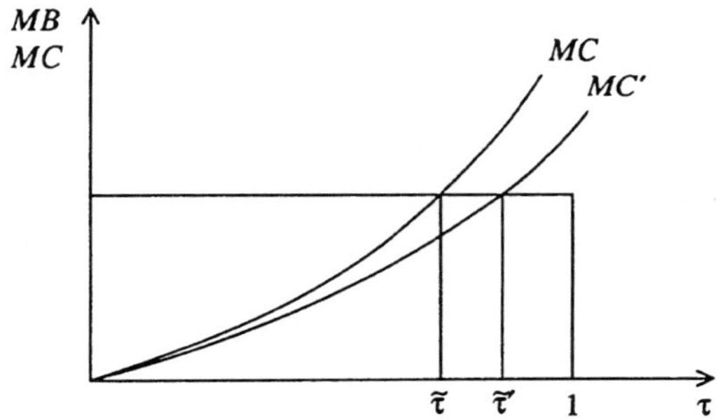

Denote by Z the marginal value of ψ associated with a complete default ($\tau = 1$). In the case of a penalty contingent upon the intensity of default we get

$$Z = hP_0/[D(1 + r^*)] \tag{39}$$

so that the borrowing country

DEFAULT IF $\psi > Z$
NOT DEFAULT IF $\psi < Z$

If $h = 1$ the default decision rule is even simpler:

$$\tau = 0 \quad \text{if} \quad \psi < P_0/D(1 + r^*)$$

$$\tau = 1 \quad \text{if} \quad \psi > P_0/D(1 + r^*)$$

which is exactly the same result one would get with a fixed default penalty (Aizenman, 1986, p.5).

Now it is interesting to see what are the welfare effects of the introduction of a variable default scheme that tie the penalty to the default rate. Before going to the algebra let us consider verbally what are these effects.

Allowance for endogenous default penalties is associated with a rise in the interest rate and thus with a rise in country risk. This is so because for a given interest rate a higher h implies, as we have seen in the previous pages (fig.4.2), a higher default rate. A higher default rate reduces the expected yield on a given volume of indebtness thus necessitating a rise in the interest rate.

A rise in the interest rate for a given level of indebtness means a leftward shift of the supply of credit and consequently a rise in country risk.

Figure 4.3
Shift in the supply of credit due to a higher default rate

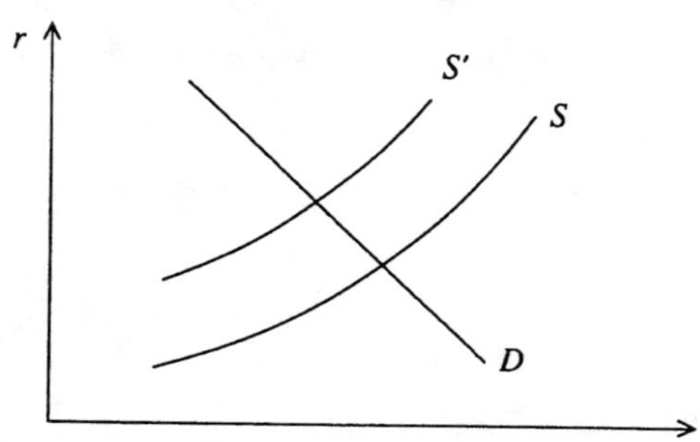

On the other hand the adverse effect of a rise in the interest rate is partly offset by the rise in the incidence of partial default associated with default income.

To see what is the global effect of an endogenous penalty we thus have to look at the effect of an increase in h on the expected utility associated with a given level of borrowing. Expected utility for a level of indebtness equal to D is

$$E(U) = u(c_1 + D) + \rho \int_{\varepsilon}^{Z} u(c_2 - D(1 + r^*) + y(\tau))g(\psi)d\psi$$

$$+ \rho \int_{\varepsilon}^{\infty} u(c_2 - P_0/\psi)g(\psi)d\psi \qquad (40)$$

where $y(\tau)$ and Z are defined in equations (38) and (39), c_1 and c_2 are endowments in period 1 and 2 respectively and g is the density function of the distribution of ψ.

Partially deriving expected utility with respect to h we get

$$\delta E(U) = - \int_{\varepsilon}^{Z} u^1(x_{1,n})\, D(1 - \tau) \frac{\delta(1 + r^*)}{\delta h} g(\psi)d\psi < 0 \qquad (41)$$

Therefore, it is possible to conclude that a greater responsiveness of the penalty scheme to the default rate results in a drop in expected welfare. As we already mentioned, this is because the introduction of a variable default cost raises the rate of expected default for a given credit volume, consequently necessitating a higher interest rate. Moreover, the indirect gains associated with the greater flexibility of the default structure are not strong enough to offset the adverse effect of the rise in interest rate.

Repayment schemes that make the default penalty contingent upon the intensity of default undertaken by the borrowing country are, thus, undesirable.

4.5 IS THE ANNOUNCEMENT OF DEBT PAYMENTS SUSPENSION A CREDIBLE ONE?

A line of argument of some interest is the one presented by Dooley and Svensson (1990). They suggest that the willingness of debtors to make external debt-service payments reflects, in part, their inability to credibly and permanently suspend debt-service. If this is so, the role that penalties will play in the repayment process is one of minor importance.

It is now important to understand what are the different effects of a permanent, compared to a temporary, suspension of debt-service payments and why investors think that the announcement of a permanent default is not a credible one.

A suspension of payments that is permanent and is believed to be permanent may cause a beneficial increase in private domestic investment because a default is viewed as a promise not to tax new investors in order to pay existing creditors.

A suspension of payments that is believed to be temporary, on the other hand, will have a very limited effect on investment and income. Moreover, investors would expect a default to be temporary since, once investment and income have increased, it may be optimal for the government of the borrowing country to renew debt-service payments. As Dooley and Svesson suggest that, "the government is expected to 'default on the default' because at higher levels of domestic income the marginal costs of resuming payments are lower as compared to the benefits of avoiding penalties".

The heart of the problem is always one of weight comparing the costs and benefits associated with the actions undertaken by the borrowers. If the suspension of debt-service payments is seen as a temporary one the benefits associated with it are low and even mild penalties may possibly offset them.

This line of argument allow Dooley and Svensson to affirm that it is for this reason that in an economic setting like the one we face, where the penalties that lenders can impose seem to be both temporary and mild, debtor countries still make substantial net transfer to creditors.

We are in a framework where the funds that necessitate debt repayments are raised through taxation.

Let D be the debt level, r the interest rate on debt, t the tax rate, $I(0 \leq I \leq I)$ investment, with I being the maximum attainable level, α the constant output – capital ratio. Income after investment is thus defined as $Y = \alpha I$; income after tax used for debt repayment as $y = (1 - t)\alpha I$ and the amount of default as $x = (1 + r)D - t\alpha I$ where $t\alpha I$ is debt repayment.

The government of the borrowing country seeks to maximise welfare as given by

$$V(t, I) = U(y) - C(x)$$

$$= U((1-t)\,\alpha I - C((1+r)D - t\alpha I \qquad (42)$$

with $Uy > 0, Uyy < 0, Cx > 0, Cxx > 0$

For what concerns the determination of investments it is assumed that, moving in a competitive world capital market, investors require that

$$(1-t)\,\alpha = (1+r^*)$$

where $(1-t)\,\alpha$ is the after tax rate of return on domestic investment and $R^* = (1+r^*)$ is a given world rate of return. Consequently equilibrium investment is a function of the tax rate:

$$I(t) = \begin{cases} I & \text{for } t \leq t^* \\ 0 & \text{for } t > t^* \end{cases} \qquad (43)$$

where t^* is the critical tax rate defined as

$$t^* = 1 - (1+r^*)/\alpha$$

For $t>t^*$, $I = 0$, $y = 0$ and x reaches its maximum value $(x = (1+r)D)$. This represents the worst possible outcome for government which certainly will restrict its choice to $t \leq t^*$ (so that $I = I$ and $y > 0$).

Hence the government chooses to maximise (42) subject to $t \leq t^*$.

First order conditions give for an optimum $t = t$

$$U_y((1-t)\alpha I) \leq C_x((1+r)D - t\alpha I)\; t \leq t^* \qquad (44)$$

Equation (44) becomes an equality when $t < t^*$. We can now represent graphically the marginal utility of income after tax and the marginal cost of default (fig.4.4).[9]

Figure 4.4
Marginal utility, marginal cost and the determination of equilibrium tax rate

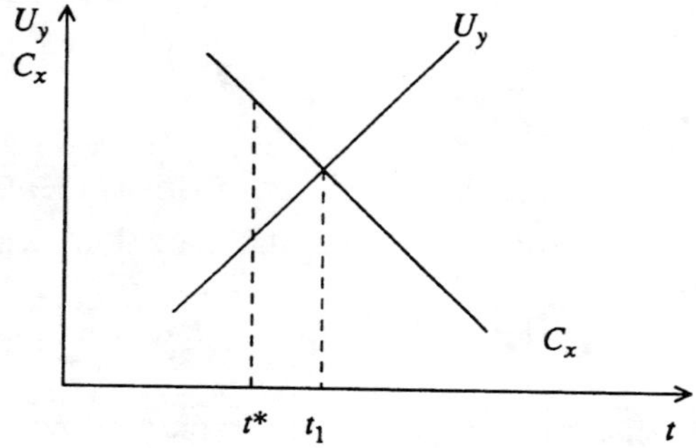

Marginal utility equals marginal cost for a tax rate equal to t_1.

Now

$$\text{IF } t^* > t_1 \Leftrightarrow t = t_1 \text{ is the optimal tax rate}$$
$$\text{IF } t^* < t_1 \Leftrightarrow t = t^* \text{ is the optimal tax rate}$$

We have to notice that when $t = t^*$ marginal utility falls short of the marginal cost.

But what happens if we allow the government to re-optimise after international investors have committed themselves to I believing that the government will choose a tax rate $t = t^*$. Once the investors have committed themselves to the maximum level of investment I the constraint $t \leq t^*$ loses its relevance and the government will choose $t = t_1$ so as to equate marginal utility and marginal cost. The after tax rate of return on investment will fall short of the world rate of interest, but for investors would be impossible or costly to change their decisions.

So the conclusion is that if investors act rationally they will anticipate the increase in the tax rate and choose not to invest at all. This will mean for the government maximum default!

NOTES

1. Gersovitz, M. (1986), p.62
2. Sachs, J. (1984); Krugman, P. (1986); Fernandez, R. and Glazer, J. (1989).
3. For a general discussion on legal, institutional and political issues see Kaletsky (1985); on U.S. legislation see Eaton and Gersovitz (1981).
4. We must remember, however, that under certain circumstances the lender country may impound the borrowing country's reserves. See also Bulow, J. and Rogoff, K. (1989).
5. This allows the aggregation of all firms into a single one whose production technology is the sum of individual technologies.
6. As we have already mentioned, even when the creditors can seize assets belonging to any resident of the country, defaulting on the debt will still be collectively superior if the country is a net debtor. So only an additional penalty can deter default.
7. It is only a threat the lender can impose on a country which would default.
8. Since optimal taxation is not a topic of direct interest for this book, readers who wish to follow the analysis further can refer to Cohen (1989), pp.43–46.
9. The marginal utility curve is positively sloped because as the tax rate t falls, after-tax income rises and the marginal utility of consumption falls. The marginal cost curve on the other hand is negatively sloped because as t falls, the amount of default rises and the marginal cost imposed on the debtor increases.

5 Credit rationing on the sovereign loan market and the possibility of a total breakdown of lending

5.1 CREDIT RATIONING

In equilibrium, credit markets may be characterised by rationing (Stiglitz and Weiss, 1983). Credit rationing means the existence of an excess demand for loanable funds. Price adjustments (interest rate changes) cannot be used to eliminate the excess demand, because the price itself affects borrowers' behaviour.

We are in a world where different borrowers have different probabilities of repaying their loan. Since the expected return to the bank depends on the probability of repayment, it is crucial for the bank to identify borrowers that are more likely to repay. This would be easy given perfect information about borrowers, but in the credit market some degree of imperfect information is the rule, and therefore the bank is not able to stipulate precisely all the actions the borrower could take. It is for that reason that the bank may decide to use the interest rate as a screening device. The reasoning is that those who are willing to borrow at high interest rates are willing to do that because they perceive their probability of repaying the loan to be low. A higher interest rate means higher risk, hence possibly lower profits.

If we trace the expected return to the bank with respect to the interest rate the shape of the function looks like the one in Figure 5.1.

Figure 5.1
The relationship between expected return and interest rate

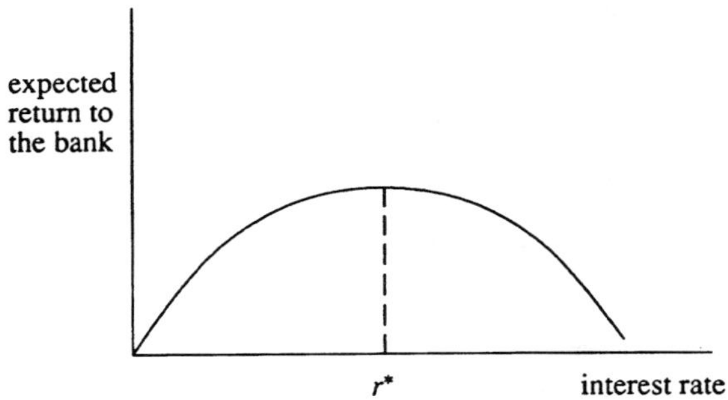

In the figure, r^* is the interest rate that maximises the bank's expected return.

It is possible that at r^* the demand for funds exceeds the supply, but even if the market does not clear r^* is the equilibrium interest rate since the bank would not lend to an individual who offered to pay more than r^*. There are no forces leading supply to equal demand, and credit is rationed.

Debt problems may be interpreted as the consequence of a breakdown in the normal process of achieving equilibrium in the market for foreign credit and therefore as a consequence of credit rationing.

As we have seen, when lenders have imperfect information about borrowers they may consider the interest rate the borrower is prepared to pay as an informational proxy for soundness. So it may happen that beyond some ceiling established by normal practice, the lender will be unwilling to lend more in return for a higher interest rate, because a higher interest rate means worse risk.

Accordingly, the supply of international loans turns totally inelastic with respect to interest rates once this ceiling rate is reached. It may also happen that in correspondence to the ceiling rate the amount a country seeks to borrow exceeds the amount that foreign banks are prepared to supply.

Figure 5.2
Credit rationing with the market in disequilibrium

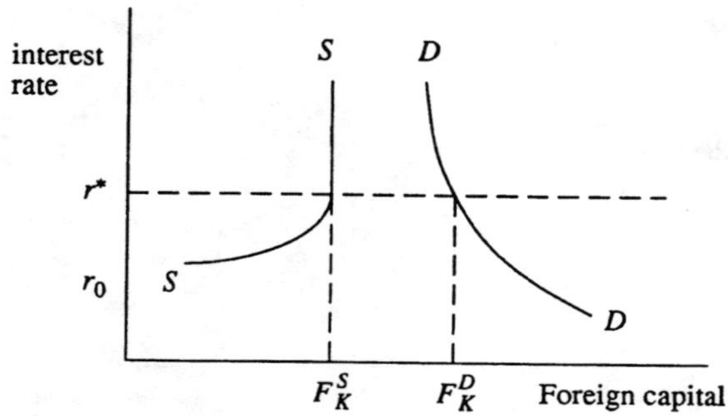

In Figure 5.2, at a ceiling interest rate r^* the amount of foreign loans demanded equals FK^D and the amount supplied is FK^S. The market is in disequilibrium, and credit is rationed.

5.1.1 Credit rationing in Heffernan's model

In the model developed by Heffernan (1986), described in Chapter 3, two independent sources of potential credit rationing are identified: a high return on the safe asset when lenders are risk-neutral and a high degree of risk aversion.

In deriving the supply of foreign loans, Heffernan assumes that lender countries could invest excess capital in two different assets: a sovereign loan to developing countries, perceived as risky because of the possibility of default, and a safe domestic asset with zero probability of default. Moreover, the model assumes the possibility of two different states of the world obtaining: a good state, when all of the sovereign loan is repaid, and a bad state, when the borrowing country repays only a proportion q of principal and interests.

5.1.2 Lenders maximise expected utility

In the special case of risk neutrality the expected utility for lenders is given by

$$E(U) = W[\alpha(1 + r_s) + (1 - \alpha)[\pi(1 + r) + (1 - \pi)q]] \tag{1}$$

where W is the initial wealth of the lender country, π is the probability of the good state obtaining, α is the proportion of W held in the safe domestic asset, r is the interest rate on the risky asset and r_s the interest rate on the safe asset.

From the first order conditions for the maximisation of expected utility we get

$$1 + r_s = \pi(1 + r) + (1 - \pi)q \tag{2}$$

We are now able to derive an explicit expression for the probability of default.

$$1 - \pi = \frac{r - r_s}{1 + r - q} \tag{3}$$

Using equation (3) it is possible to analyse the way in which the interest rate on the risky asset influences the probability of default.

Suppose the existence of two limit values for the risky interest rate, r_1 and r_2, $r_1 < r_2$.

If the interest rate is sufficiently low, $r < r_1$, default never occurs. For $r > r_2$ default is a certainty.

Between r_1 and r_2 the probability of default is assumed to be linear in r:

$$\pi = \max[\min(h, 1), \max(h, 0)] \tag{4}$$

where $$h = \frac{r_2 - r}{r_2 - r_1}$$

Consequently between r_1 and r_2 the expected yield on the risky asset (call it ψ), given by the right hand side of equation 2, is quadratic:

$$\psi = -\frac{1}{r_2 - r_1} r^2 + \frac{r_2 + q - 1}{r_2 - r_1} r + \frac{r_2 - r_1 q}{r_2 - r_1} \qquad (5)$$

This function will have a maximum at the point

$$r = \frac{r_2 + q - 1}{2}$$

Figure 5.3
The rate of interest and the expected return on risky loans

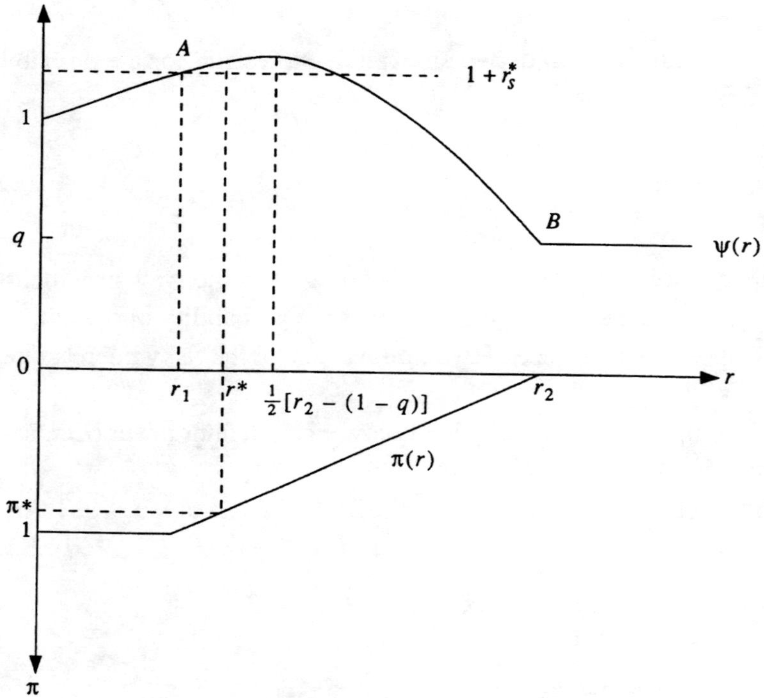

Let us now assume that the interest rate on the safe asset, r_s, equals r_s^*.

From equation 2 we know that the yield on the two assets must have the same mathematical expectation. The risky asset must therefore yield an interest equal to r_s and the probability of default associated with it must be $(I - \pi)^*$:

$$1 + r_s^* = \pi^*(1 + r^*) + (1 - \pi^*)q \qquad (6)$$

The two possible solutions for r will be:

$$\text{if } r_s \leqslant r_1 \quad \Rightarrow \quad r = r_s$$

$$\text{if } r_s > r_1 \quad \Rightarrow \quad r = \frac{r_2 + q - 1}{2} + \\ - \sqrt{\frac{(1 - q + r_2)^2}{4} + r_1(1 - q) - r_s(r_2 - r_1)} \qquad (7)$$

For low values of r_s the expression under the square root operator will be positive and there will be an r,

$$r < \frac{r_2 - (1 - q)}{2}$$

for which equation 2 will be satisfied. For high values of r_s, on the other hand, the expression under square root will be negative and the imaginary solution for r corresponds to the case where risky loans vanish.

Heffernan (1985) concludes that "if r_s lies at or below the rate at which default disappears as a possibility, r will equal r_s. If r_s is so high that risky loans cannot promise the same expected yield at any r, risky loans will disappear: it does not pay the investor to purchase the risky asset because the yield on the safe asset is so high. This is a case of potential credit rationing".

A second case of potential credit rationing envisaged by the model is given by the assumption of a risk-aversion coefficient equal to unity,

$c = 1$, and of $\pi(r)$ taking the bounded linear form assumed earlier:

$$\pi(r) = \max[\min(h, 1), \max(h, 0)], \; h = \frac{r_2 - r}{r_2 - r_1}$$

Starting from the sovereign loan supply equation derived earlier

$$L = W \frac{(1 + r_s)(1 - F)}{FZ_1 + Z_z} \tag{8}$$

where $Z_1 = r - r_s$

$$Z_2 = 1 + r_s - q$$

$$F = \left(\frac{1 - \pi}{\pi} \frac{Z_2}{Z_1}\right)^{1/c}$$

we can derive the elasticity of L with respect to r. We get

$$e_{L,r} = \eta \left[\frac{r}{Z_1}\left(\frac{Z_2}{Z_1} + 1 - c(1 - F) + \frac{\tilde{\pi}}{1 - \pi}(1 + \frac{Z_2}{Z_1})\right)\right] \tag{9}$$

where $\tilde{\pi}$ is the elasticity of π to r which in our case equals

$$\tilde{\pi} = -[1/(r_2 - r)] \tag{10}$$

Knowing that and c being equal to 1, we can solve for the critical value of r at which the supply of loans is infinitely elastic

$$r = r_s + \sqrt{r_2^2 + (r_s - r_1)(1 - q)} \tag{11}$$

This can be described as a second case of possible credit rationing.

If $r > r_s + \sqrt{r_2^2 + (r_s - r_1)(1 - q)}$ any further increase in r will result in a reduction in the willingness to lend (i.e. the supply curve bends backward).

Figure 5.4
The backward bending supply of foreign loans

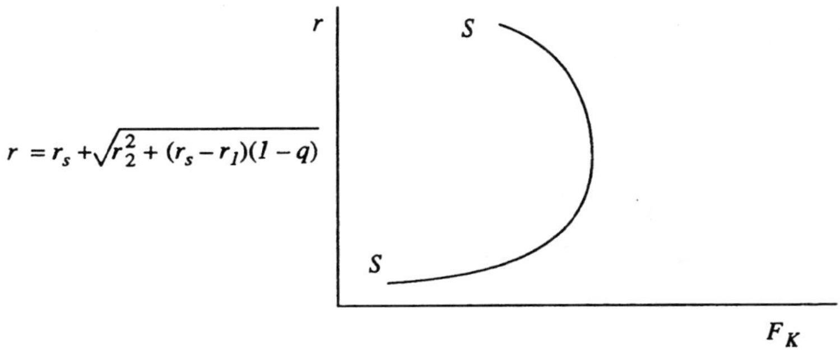

In this case the possibility that foreign loans may dry up entirely is due to the presence of a strong risk aversion.

5.1.3 Asymmetric information about exposures and credit rationing

The interest rate a country is prepared to pay, however, is not the only variable that is important in determining borrower behaviour. The amount borrowed is also relevant.

In "Asymmetries on information and LDC borrowing with sovereign risk" (1984) Kletzer assumes asymmetrical information between debtors and creditors. Borrowers have more information than lenders about the total amount of debt they have undertaken.

In analysing the properties of competitive equilibria in loan contracts under alternative assumptions about the information possessed by creditors, we make the following assumptions: that production is stochastic, that debtors maximise the discounted stream of expected utility from consumption in each period under the constraint that a default leads to an embargo on future credit, and that creditors maximise expected profits. On this basis, a number of observations can be made. If lenders are unable to know the system's total exposure to a borrower, then debtor countries with different concurrent indebtedness cannot be distinguished. An equilibrium may or may not exist (Figures 5.5, 5.6).

Figure 5.5
The existence of an equilibrium in the loan market

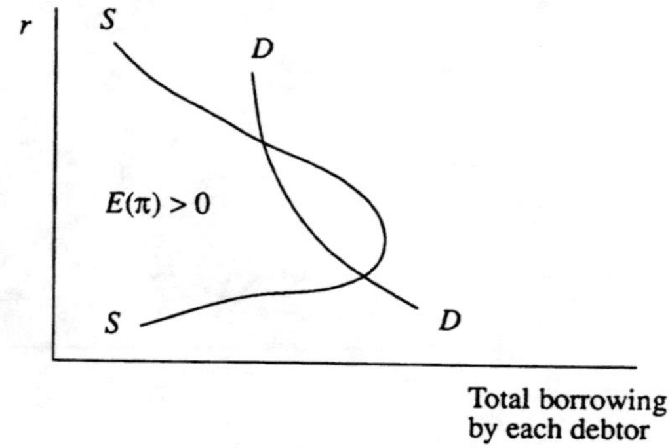

Figure 5.6
The non-existence of an equilibrium in the loan market

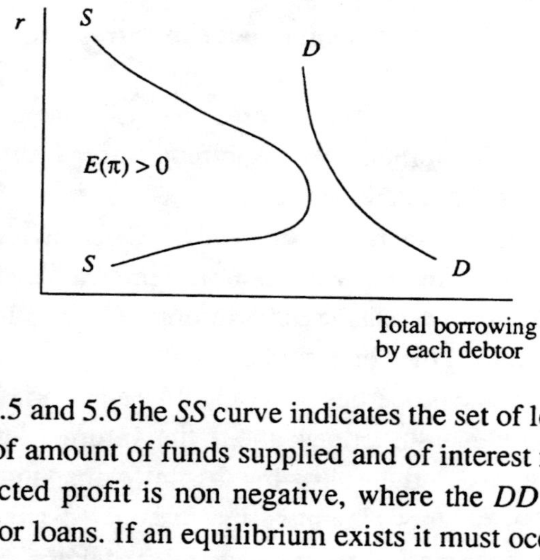

In Figures 5.5 and 5.6 the *SS* curve indicates the set of loan contracts (combinations of amount of funds supplied and of interest rate charged) for which expected profit is non negative, where the *DD* curve is the demand curve for loans. If an equilibrium exists it must occur along the demand curve, and the interest rate alone can be used to ration loans.

If on the other hand lenders are informed of each debtor's total borrowing at each date, then loan contracts specifying the rate of interest to be paid as a function of total borrowing are possible. Moreover competition will assure a loan-interest rate combination that maximizes the borrower utility subject to the non-negative profit condition. The equilibrium is consequently determined by the tangency of a borrower's indifference curve to the supply curve (Figure 5.7)

Figure 5.7
Equilibrium with credit rationing in the loan market

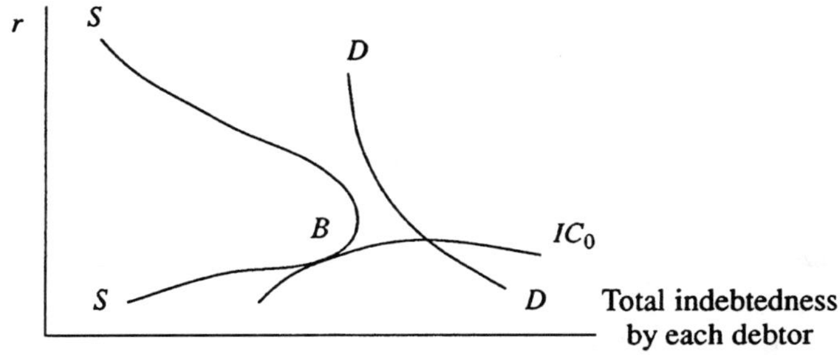

Indicating with IC_o an indifference curve of the borrower over loan contracts, equilibrium will be at point B in Figure 6 and will typically[1] entail credit rationing (i.e. equilibrium contracts occur inside the demand curve) and the borrower will be constrained in that, given the interest rate, he would prefer to borrow more.

Figure 5.8, depicting equilibriums both with and without lender knowledge of the borrower's overall position, implies that the equilibrium without such observability, if it exists, is characterized by a higher debt and a higher interest rate (point A) than if total debt is observable (point B).

Figure 5.8
Equilibriums with and without observability of the borrower's overall position

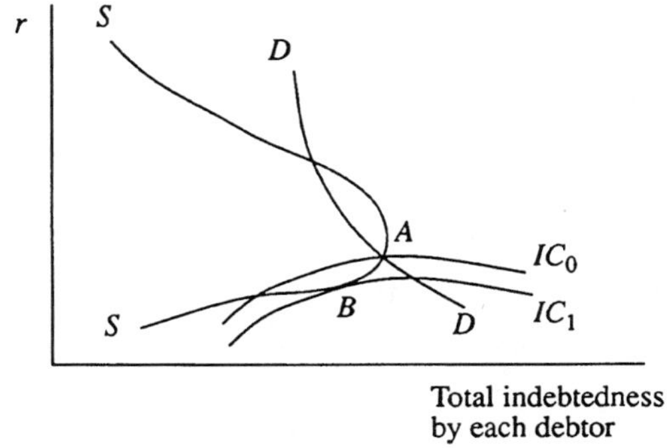

The conclusion is that the borrower is better off when its debt position is observable, since the lower rate of interest more than compensates for the rationing of credit.

5.2 A TOTAL HALT IN LENDING

The imperfect information models we considered allow for lenders to deal with these problems at least well enough to justify some lending. On the other hand, it is possible to hypothesize a total collapse of loan supply if lenders are unable to cope with enforcement problems or if a panic occurs.

In the first instance the breakdown in lending is caused by lenders' inability to commit themselves to a pre-established ceiling on indebtedness. In the second case, market failure results from the rational behaviour of a large number of small lenders. Each bank's decisions about its financing to a borrower country depend in part on the actions of other banks. If, for example, a borrowing country suffers a short-run fall in income and needs a large loan to tide it over, it may happen that all banks but one stop lending. Thus only a very large loan from the remaining bank may save the borrower from default. But if each bank faces an increasing cost of lending or if the risk increases with the amount lent, it becomes unprofitable or too risky for the remaining bank to supply the requisite funds. If no other bank steps in, this last remaining bank may also decide to stop lending, and a total halt in lending will occur.

Let us now look at the first, possible cause of a breakdown of lending: the inability of lenders to establish a ceiling on indebtedness.

Given imperfect information, past failure is interpreted as a signal of probable future failure. In a perfect-information world, on the other hand, there may be an incentive to throw good money after bad. In other words, a naive cut-off behaviour may not actually be in creditors' interest.

Hellwig (1977) develops a model in which each borrowing country is given a credit limit. The debtor goes bankrupt and suffers a fixed penalty if the debt reaches the limit and it cannot pay the interest.

At the beginning of the period the borrowing country has zero income but at some unknown future date income is expected to jump. If the borrower exhausts the initial line of credit before its income rises, the lender has an incentive to provide more. Cutting off finance would mean the default of the borrowing country, hence no repayment for the lender. Extending additional credit means, for the lender, some hope of repayment. Consequently, it is important to distinguish between the case in which the lender succeeds in setting an inviolable ceiling on the credit extended and the case in which, fearing default, decides to supply additional funds.

If the lender could set a rigid ceiling on its exposure, a loan to a country would provide a non-negative expected yield. If additional funds are supplied to the debtor to ward off default, these funds would not yield a positive expected return *per se;* nevertheless, the overall situation may still be such that it pays the lender to throw good money after bad, to recover at least part of that earlier investment

Now, it may be the case that debtors anticipate the behaviour of creditors regarding their request for additional loans. If the debtor country knows that the creditor will supply additional funds, it will draw down the initial amount of credit more quickly, increasing the probability of going bankrupt before its income rises.

By initially extending credit, then, the lender places himself in a situation in which the commitment of additional funds may be profitable even when the expected return on all the funds committed is negative. For this reason the lender may refuse to lend at all, and a breakdown in lending occurs.

The possibility of a breakdown exists because the creditor is unable to control his own future lending behaviour or the borrower's consumption once the loan has been made. This second aspect is relevant since the rate of consumption of the borrowing country determines how soon the credit limit is reached, which in turn influences the probability of insolvency. We are back to a moral hazard problem, which enters with the assumption that the debtor country is free to determine its rate of consumption.

As was pointed out above, another potential cause of a halt to lending is a sudden loss of confidence by creditors, who consequently decide to withdraw capital and abandon a possibly profitable loan.

Such a loss of confidence and credit run has some similarity, as noted by Eaton, Gersovitz and Stiglitz (1986), to bank runs when depositors all suddenly withdraw their money. In the case of foreign loans, the borrowing country assumes the role of the banks and the lending banks that of the individual depositors.

A credit run of this sort requires the existence of one borrower and many creditors. In Sachs's model (1984) on the supply side there is a large number of banks, each with an upward sloping schedule of loan supplies to the borrowing country: individual banks face an increasing marginal cost of lending.

We can consequently write the inverse supply schedule of bank i as

$$E(r_{Fi}) = w + f(D_i/K_i) \tag{15}$$

where $E(r_{Fi})$ is the expected return on a foreign loan to bank i; D_i is the amount of the bank's total lending to the country; K_i is the bank's total capital.

A loan supply schedule like equation (15) can be derived assuming risk aversion on the part of the investor bank, which seeks to maximize utility and applying a capital asset pricing model approach of the sort illustrated in chapter 2. According to (15), the return required on a loan to a developing country will be close to w when the loan is a small fraction of the bank total capital. The expected return demanded by a bank increases as the loan represents a larger and larger share of total capital.

Equation (15) shows that there is a strong incentive for loan diversification among a large number of creditors.

If a single bank makes a loan of size $d = D_i/K_i$, the borrowing country has to pay an expected return of

$$E(r_{Fi}) = w + f(d) \tag{16}$$

If the same size loan is equally divided among N banks, the rate of return to be paid by the borrowing country will be

$$E(r_{Fi}) = w + f(d/N) \tag{17}$$

So consequently, the cost of borrowing will decrease as the number of creditors increases. As the number of banks participating in the loan tends to infinity ($N \to \infty$) the cost of borrowing tends to w.

Next let us analyze why creditors may get into a panic. Assume a two-period framework. In the first period a country has obligations given by

$$\text{DEBT OBLIGATION 1st PERIOD} = (1 + r_1)D_1 \tag{18}$$

and current income of a

$$Y_1 < (1 + r_1)\,D_1 \tag{19}$$

In the second period the income of the borrowing country is stochastic and will equal y with probability π or zero with probability $(I - \pi)$:

$$\begin{cases} y_2 = y & \textit{with PROBABILITY } \pi \\ y_2 = 0 & \textit{with PROBABILITY } (1 - \pi) \end{cases} \tag{20}$$

Assuming that debt is highly diversified among creditors, each bank's expected return will be

$$E(r_{Fi}) = w \tag{21}$$

Since in the first period current income is less than total obligations, in the second period the country should borrow and the amount of debt will be

$$D_2 \geq (1 + r_1) D_1 - Y_1 \tag{22}$$

New credit must yield at least r_2, where r_2 is such that

$$\pi(1 + r_2) = 1 + w$$

and

$$(1 + r_2) = (1 + w)/\pi$$

so that new creditors are satisfied.

Now we may distinguish three cases

1. if $\underline{y} \leq (1 + r_2) D_2$ or, in terms of D_1,

   if $\underline{y} \leq (1 + w)[(1 + r_1)D_1 - Y_1]/\pi$

2. if $\lambda y < (1 + w)[(1 + r_1)D_1 - Y_1]/\pi$ the country defaults because the repudiation risk precludes new loans.

3. if $\lambda y > (1 + w)[(1 + r_1)D_1 - Y_1]/\pi$ the country can obtain new loans on a competitive basis.

The case we are interested in is that in which all banks suddenly expect all other banks to stop lending to the country. In the light of that expectation it will be rational, for certain parameter values, to stop lending. In this way the expectation becomes self-fulfilling and a total breakdown in lending, a credit run, may result.

Consequently the borrowing country may find itself in a situation where even in the third-case framework, it is nevertheless unable to obtain new loans.

Let us now analyse what happens step by step. Consider a single bank planning its loans under the assumption of no loans from other banks.

What is certain is that, unless the bank decides to lend

$$D_2 = (1 + r_1) D_1 - Y_1 \tag{23}$$

the borrowing country will default.

Referring to the inverse supply schedule (15), we know that a single loan of size D_2 must yield an expected return of

$$E(r_{2F}) = w + f(D_2/K) \tag{24}$$

Since the debtor can only hope to be paid off in the second period with probability π, the interest rate must at least be such that

$$\pi(1 + r_2) = 1 + w + f(D_2/K) \tag{25}$$

Then, going back to case 3 it is possible to say that a liquidity crisis may arise if

$$[1 + w + f(D_2/K)]D_2/\pi > \lambda y > (1 + w)D_2/\pi \tag{26}$$

where D_2 is given by equation (23).

The case analysed brings us to the conclusion that for many banks it would be safe to lend, but lending would not be safe at all for any single bank. The risk premium required for the individual bank is such as to push the country to debt repudiation in the next period.

Hence, if all banks believe that all other banks will stop lending, a panic will arise and the breakdown of lending will occur.

Sachs (1984), however, stresses that a panic requires a fairly high level of initial debt. In particular, it is possible to affirm that a panic requires:

$$[1 + r_{2F}(D_2)]D_2 > \lambda y \tag{27}$$

It is also possible to recognize a critical value for D_2, D_2^{MIN}, for which if $D_2 \leq D_2^{MIN}$ a panic is impossible and if $D_2 \geq D_2^{MIN}$ a panic can occur.

Consequently the individual supply schedule can be represented as shown in Figure 5.9 and for $D_2 > D_2^{MIN}$, r_{2F} is such that $(1 + r_2)D_2 > \lambda y$.

Figure 5.9
The relationship between a panic occuring and the interest rate

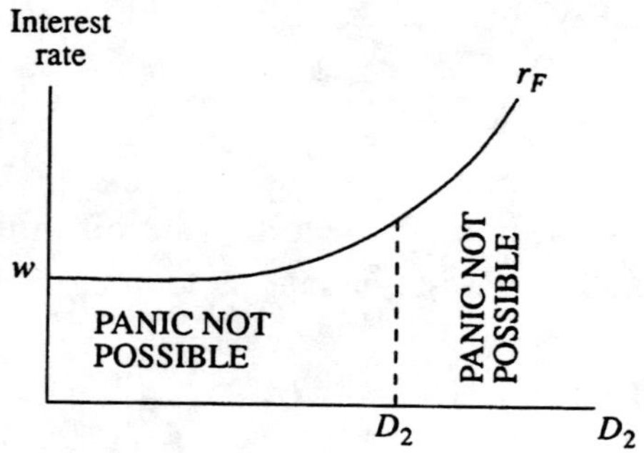

NOTES

1. For special cases look at Kletzer (1984), pp.296–8.

6 Recent developments in the theory of country risk

In the late 1980's the focus of country risk analysis moved to the question of what to do with developing countries' debts.

Economists did not want to speculate any longer on the causes of debt problems analysing the demand and supply of foreign loans, but wanted to concentrate their intellectual efforts in analysing how could developing countries could surmount the crisis.

Everything begun with the recognition that the heavily indebted developing countries could not repay all of their debt. The substantial discount that took place at the end of the 1980's was an evident and clear sign of the fact that lenders did not expect to get back the face value of their claims.

Moreover, the "public good" (or public bad!!) nature of sovereign debt was recognised. Lending countries understood that they could not simply wait for the banks and the debtors to find their own way out of the crisis. In 1989 Cohen wrote, "whichever lending or borrowing side of the coin is considered, all parties must acknowledge that sovereign debt has ceased to be a strictly private matter".

From this follows the call for all increasing government involvement in the debt crisis. In the United States the Brady Plan[1], as already the previous Baker Plan[2] wanted a deeper involvement of U.S. government in the crisis and tried to give criteria according to which public money has to be allocated to get to a resolution of the crisis itself.

The new key word in the Brady Plan was: debt reduction.

But how can a debt reduction be obtained? According to the Brady Plan, debt reductions can be obtained through the implementation of policies consisting of arrangements under which the international institutions would lend to permit less-developed countries' governments to negotiate purchase of their debt to commercial banks at a deep discount.

It is interesting to notice the different approach to a solution of the debt crisis proposed by the Brady Plan as compared with the one proposed by the Baker plan.

The key idea underlying the Baker Plan was that countries would receive new lending from the banks and the official creditors in return for undertaking programs of economic adjustment and reform. These bank lending packages became known as "new money packages".

The Baker Plan identified the insufficient supply of credit as the main cause of the debt crisis, where the Brady approach postulated instead that the debt was already too large and that it had to be scaled down if any resumption of growth was to be expected. In other words, too large a debt acts as a too large a tax in the Laffer curve setting, creating a disincentive to grow: lenders will be trapped on the right hand side of the Laffer curve if they do not realise that insisting on too great a payment can be counter-productive.

So economists started to develop lines of argument in support and against sovereign debt repurchases versus programs of direct investments or versus conditional lending programs.

The point of discussion can be summarised as follows: it is better to use resources of the international institutions and national assistance agencies to retire debt or it is better to make these resources available, as new money, to finance investment?

In this framework, the first question economists have to answer to is why there should be any difference over the intermediate run between debt forgiveness and the granting of an equivalent amount of new credits.

Sachs (1986, 1989) gives a good analytical underpinning for debt forgiveness. According to him the debt of developing countries is selling at a discount in the secondary market because "they can not pay it back". Investors, in light of the debt overhang[3] prefer not to undertake otherwise profitable investments since the entire increment of output will go to additional debt repayments.

Sachs (1986) demonstrates that both lenders and debtors may gain from some write-down of the debt. In other words debtors may find that consuming rather than investing can be in their best interests since creditors would be the main beneficiaries of the return from investment.

Krueger (1980, pp.15–19) however is critical of Sachs view. First of all she asserts that it is not necessarily the entire increment of output obtained by increased investment which has to accrue to creditors. Moreover, she argues that the degree to which the secondary market appropriately reflects the present value of future payments on debt for heavily indebted countries is questionable. Basically she questions the abstract terms in which the ability to pay of the debtor countries is defined. She takes the example of a country having mineral assets with present value in excess of the face value of the debt. Even if it is easy to understand that for a country it is politically unthinkable to sell its natural resources, the example chosen makes it clear that when evaluating the ability to pay of a debtor country political realities have greater weight than any inherent ability to service debt. Consequently the price of debt in the secondary market should be regarded more as a "market valuation of the probability of a government's undertaking appropriate policy measures than as a government's ability to service debt".

Secondly Krueger gives several explanations of why "new money" when heavily orientated toward investment is preferable if compared with new money orientated toward resources freed by debt relief. She asserts that "some ground exists for believing that if the World bank lends, for example, to construct additional power facilities in a heavily indebted country which is subject to extreme pressure to reduce its government spending, then investment is likely to be greater than it would be if the World Bank instead lends for debt relief".

Dooley (1983) on the other hand affirms that it need not always be the case that buy-backs are a bad deal. When the country makes a buy back which uses reserves which would otherwise have to be given at their face value to the lenders, the buy-back is in fact a good deal: whatever the discount, it is always better for the country to use one dollar of reserve to repurchase two dollars of debt rather than using that dollar to redeem one dollar of interest.

It has to be noticed however that where Krueger was not necessarily assuming that the entire increment of output created by the increased investment obtained by the use of new money has to go to debt repayment, Dooley is assuming that new money goes, directly or indirectly, to debt repayment. This makes the difference!

However, Dooley's example raises the important issue of the existing difference between the marginal and the average price of the debt.

Bulow and Rogoff (1988) in their paper "Sovereign Debt Repurchase: No Cure for Overhang" analyze the implications of a discrepancy between the marginal price of debt and its average price for buy-backs.

The marginal value of the debt can be defined as the value for the banking community as a whole of one more dollar held on a debtor country. The average price of debt is the value for an individual investor of one more dollar held on the country.

If a borrowing country wants to repurchase its debt on the secondary market it has to pay the average price where as far as the real burden of the debt is concerned it is the marginal price that is relevant.

We are back to the Dooley idea that it is always better for a country to use a dollar of reserve to repurchase two dollars of debt rather than using that dollar to redeem one dollar of interest.

A more concrete proposal is the one advanced by Cohen (1989). He wanted to outline a debt relief scheme according to which: "when a debtor generates one dollar of surplus, this dollar of "hard currency" should be "counted" as two dollars of a nominal claim on itself, if the equilibrium average price of the debt is fifty cents on the dollar" or in other words, if the "true" market price of Brazilian debt is fifty cents on the dollar then any dollar of interest paid by Brazil should be accompanied by an "interest holiday" of one dollar".

The optimal rescheduling of debt proposals which followed (Cohen, 1988) was one consisting of splitting the debt into two components: a performing and non-performing part. According to this proposal lenders should act "as if" the debt amounted to the performing component (reflecting the market value of the debt) and scale how much money the borrower should service on that part. The non-performing part need not necessarily be written down.

However, Bulow and Rogoff (1990) went on warning that "a debt discount facility would in fact be a black hole for aid funds and would yield only minimal efficiency benefits". Their criticism that open-market repurchases dissipate resources extended to all forms of such repurchases including debt-for-equity swaps.[4]

Bulow and Rogoff's contention is based on the fact that when new resources are used to repurchase at the average price the debt on the secondary market, it could very well be that this money would serve no other purpose but to raise the price of the debt and give no relief in terms of the debt burden. Moreover Bulow and Rogoff argue that, according to what has happened, once the obligations of debtor countries pass into the hands of official lenders such as the World Bank it is more unlikely that debtor countries would continue to make any significant net repayments.

So far not a definite answer has been given by economists about what is the best way to take to help heavily indebted nations to solve their debt problems. The actual situation is still a very critical and complex one and consequently the related theoretical issues could not be non-controversial.

NOTES

1. The Brady Plan was outlined by the Treasury Secretary Nicholas Brady on March 10 1989.
2. The Baker Plan is the Plan concerning the heavily indebted countries debt situation, unveiled in fall 1985 by the Secretary of Treasury James Baker III.
3. According to Paul Krugman "a country has a debt overhang problem when the expected present value of potential future resource transfers is less than its debt".

4. The standard way a debt equity swap operates is that indebted countries exchange private equity in domestic economy activities for public debt held by commercial banks.

Conclusion

The aim of this book was that of giving a general, theoretical framework for understanding under what circumstances debt problems might arise through the analysis of the determinants of the demand and supply of foreign loans.

In the seventies, even if the dictum was widespread that "countries never go insolvent the way private firms do", economists started working on country risk and many statistical models were developed for the assessment of developing countries creditworthiness and for the prediction of debt problems arising. These models are described in the first part of the book where the critiques addressed to them are also discussed. Our analysis showed that, apart from the statistical difficulties, the main defect of these models consist of the lack of a theoretical framework. Hence the need for what Eaton, Gevsovitz and Stiglitz call "a pure theory of country risk".

From this originated the idea of writing a book consisting of a general, theoretical framework of analysis. We thought that it was important to start from a careful analysis of the determinants of the supply and demand for loans to understand which are the causes of debt problems arising from the demand side and the supply side.

In the second chapter of the book a general theory for the

determination of the supply of sovereign loans is outlined taking account of the different assumptions that can be made about a banks' objective function. All through the chapter we assume that lenders treat a foreign loan like any other risky asset so that the decision to invest in such loan can be seen as part of an optimal investment portfolio decision.

The bank's objective function varies according to which economic variable it is primarily interested in.

We specified the objective function when the bank's primary interest is on return, on non-systematic or diversifiable risk, on systematic or non-diversifiable risk and on bankruptcy risk.

We derived an expression for the supply of foreign loans when the bank wants to minimise total risk, maximise expected return or minimise the probability of going bankrupt.

We considered the case where banks are both concerned with risk and return and therefore when the suppliers behaviour can be analysed by applying the mean-variance approach.

We went even further since, trying to overcome some of the problems that arose in the applicability of this approach, we also used state preference theory to derive an expression for the supply of sovereign loans.

For what concerns the demand for foreign loans, two main reasons for importing external capital are stressed in the third chapter to finance a country's development and to make possible for a country to smooth investment or consumption path over time.

We analysed the development motive in a classical framework and in the framework given by the development cycle theory of indebtness.

In both these frameworks, the demand for foreign loans is motivated by the will of a developing country of reaching a higher rate of growth. In the classical framework, the demand for loans depends on the gap between savings and investment where in the development cycle theory of indebtness the loan demand depends on GNP per capita, on the share of investment in GDP and on the interest rate (or rental rate of capital). In the consumption smoothing models, optimal borrowing is determined so as to equate the marginal utilities of consumption over time. When the demand for foreign loans is derived under the assumption of income variability and uncertainty, however, the amount of desired borrowing will sometimes depend positively on the growth rate of income but always on the standard deviation of income.

After having identified the determinants of the supply and demand of foreign loans we analysed what are the causes, from the demand side and from the supply side, of debt problems arising.

From the demand side we stressed the importance of the willingness to pay of the borrowing country. Economists used to think that developing countries did not repay their loans because they were insolvent.

The latest cases of debt problems (Brazil and Mexico 1982 for example), however, showed that the non-repayment of debt was not due to the insolvency of the borrowing country but to a precise decision taken by the country of suspending payments.

Underlying the decision of honouring the debt contract is a weightening of the costs and benefits of doing so. Before defaulting on its debt, a country must carefully balance the pluses and minuses of its decision.

The costs of default can be identified in: the possible cost of access to trade credit; the risk of seizure of a country's foreign assets; the possibility of trade becoming more difficult; domestic financial instability.

The modelling of these costs or penalties is still one of the major theoretical issue country risk economists are faced with. What seems to be true is that "however large the costs of default may be, they will never be infinite. Hence there will always be some level of debt which a sovereign debtor will default on rather than servicing it in full. This may happen even though the country may well have the resources needed to service the debt" (Cohen 1989).

From the supply side we stressed the unsecured nature of sovereign loans and analysed what are the direct consequences of the absence of a collateral on which lenders can mortgage their loan.

We studied the case when the supply of foreign loan is backward bending and when it falls short of the demand so to cause credit rationing. We analysed the inefficiency of credit market when the total amount borrowed by developing countries can not be observed and when lenders lack the capability of committing themselves to a lending policy. We investigated the game between small banks and large banks and considered the risk of a panic occurring.

In the last chapter we examined the efforts made by economists to find a possible solution to the developing countries debt crisis.

We described the analytical tools of debt restrictions and debt repurchases. We discussed the debt forgiveness issue and considered the actual convenience of making direct investment in heavily indebted nations.

Of course, more can be said on all these issues and on others that this book does not include. We hope, however, that this book can be a useful guide for economists or students who want to familiarise themselves with country risk and the connected issues.

One point to be stressed is how the gap between theory and practice has not been yet fulfilled. The models used for predicting the possibility of debt problems arising still lack of a theoretical structure. Where the more and more sophisticated theoretical works on country risk which, by analysing the demand and supply of foreign loans under different assumptions, try to explain what is happening in the real world, can very seldom be subject to estimation and used for predictions.

Bibliography

Abassi, B. and Taffler, R.J. (1982), 'Country Risk: a Model of Economic Performance Related to Debt Servicing Capacity', City University Business School Working Paper.

Aizenhan, J. (1986), *Country Risk and Incentive Schemes'*, University of Chicago Working Paper, November.

Alexander, L.S. (1987), *Three Essays on Sovereign Default and International Lendings*, Ph.D. Dissertation, Yale University.

Amemiya, T. (1981), 'Qualitative Response Models: a Survey', *Journal of Economic Literature*.

Armendaziz de Aghion (1990), 'International Debt: An Explanation of the Commercial Banks' Lending Behavior After 1982', *Journal of International Economics*.

Arrow, K. (1970), 'Essay in the Theory of Risk Bearing', Markham, Chicago.

Avramovic, D. *et. al.*, (1964), Economic Growth and External Debt, John Hopkins Press, Baltimore.

Beenstock, M. (1984), *The World Economy in Transition*, Allen and Unwin, London.

Beenstock, M. and Dalziel, A. (1983), 'Economic Development and Third World Indebtness' City University Business School Seminar paper.

Bulow, J.I. and Rogoff, K. (1986), 'A Constant Recontracting Model of Sovereign Debt', NBER Working Paper No. 2088, National Bureau of Economic Research, Cambridge, Mass.

Bulow, J. and Rogoff, K. (1988), 'The Buyback Boondoggle', *Brooking Papers on Economic Activity*.

Bulow, J. and Rogoff, K. (1989), 'Sovereign Debt: Is to Forgive to Forget?', *American Economic Review*.

Bulow, J. and Rogoff, K. (1989), *Sovereign Debt Repurchase: No Cure for Overhang*, Working paper.

Bulow, J. and Rogoff, K. (1990), 'Cleaning up Third World Debt Without Getting Taken to the Cleaners', *Journal of Economic Perspectives*, Winter.
Calverley, J. and O'Brien, R. eds. (1987), *Finance and the International Economy*, Oxford University Press, Oxford.
Chenery, H. and Strout, A. (1966), 'Foreign Assistance and Economic Development', *American Economic Review.*
Cizauskas, A.C. (1979), 'International Debt Renegotiation: Lessons from the Past', *World Development.*
Clifton, E.V. (1982), 'Debtor-Creditor Games: an Approach to International Debt Renegotiations' Federal Reserve Bank of New York Research Paper no.8232, New York.
Cline, W.R. (1983), 'International Debt and The Stability of The World Economy', Institute for International Economics, Policy Analysis in International Economics no.4, Washington, DC.
Cline, W.R. (1984), *International Debt: Systematic Risk and Policy Response*, Institute For International Economics, Washington, DC.
Cohen, D. 'Is the Discount on the Secondary Market a Case for LDC Debt Relief', CEPREMAP, no.8823.
—— 'Domestic and External Debt Constraints of LDCs', in *Global Macroeconomics*, Bryant and Portès eds. Macmillan, London.
—— 'The Management of Developing Countries' Debt: Guidelines and Application to Brazil', *World Bank Economic Review.*
—— (1985), 'Inflation, Wealth and Interest Rates in an Intertemporal Optimizing Model', *Journal of Monetary Economics.*
—— (1985), 'How to Evaluate the Solvency of an Indebted Nation?', *Economic Policy*, no.1.
Cohen, D. and Sachs, J. (1986), 'Growth and External Debt under Risk of Debt Repudiation', *European Economic Review.*
Cohen, D. and Ph. Michel (1988), 'How Should Control Theory be Used by a Time-Consistent Government?', *Review of Economic Studies.*
Cohen, D. and Portes, R. (1989), 'On the Brady Plan', *Mimeo.*
Collins, R.A. and Green, R.D. (1982), 'Statistical Methods for Bankruptcy Forecasting', *Journal of Economics and Business.*
Cooper, R.N. and Sachs, J.D. (1985), 'Borrowing Abroad: the Debtor's Perspective' in Gordon, W.S. and Cuddington J. Teds. *International Debt and The Developing Countries*, IBRD, Washington D.C., pp.21–60.
Copeland, T.E. and Weston J.F. (1988) Third edition *Financial Theory and Corporate Policy*, Addison-Wesley Publishing Company, New York.
Corden, M. and Dooley, M.P. (1989), 'Issues in Debt Strategy: An Overview', in J.A. Frenkel, M.P. Dooley, and P. Wickham, eds., *Analytical Issues in Debt*, International Monetary Fund, Washington, pp.10–37.
Cox, D.R. (1970), The Analysis of Binary Data, :Methuen & Co. Ltd, London.
Cuddington, J.T. and Smith, G.W. (1985), *International Debt and the Developing Countries*, The World Bank, Washington, D.C.
Davis, R.R. (1981), 'Alternative Techniques for Country Risk Evaluation', *Business Economics.*

De Vries, B. (1971), 'The Debt Bearing Capacity of Developing Countries – a Comparative Analysis', *Banca Nazionale del Lavoro Quarterly Review.*

Dhonte, P. (1974), 'Quantitative Indicators and Analysis of External Debt Problems', International Monetary Fund mimeo, Washington, D.C.

Dhonte, P. (1975), 'Describing External Debt Situations: A Roll-Over Approach', IMF Staff Papers, vol.22, no.1, pp.159–86.

Dhonte, P. (1979), *Clockwork Debt,* D.C. Heath and Co. Lexington, Mass.

Diamond, D. and Dybuig, P. (1983), 'Bank Runs, Deposit Insurance and Liquidity', *Journal of Political Economy.*

Diaz-Alejandro, C.F. (1985), 'Goodbye Financial Repression, Hello Financial Crash', *Journal of Development Economics.*

Domar, E.D. (1950), 'The Effect of Foreign Investment On The Balance of Payments', *American Economic Review.*

Domar, E. (1944), 'The Burden of Debt and National Income', *American Economic Review.*

Dooley, H. and Svensson, L.E. (1990), 'Policy Inconsistency and External Debt Service', IMF Working Paper, April.

Eaton, J. (1990), 'Debt Relief and International Enforcement of Loan Contracts', *Journal of Economic Perspectives*, Winter.

Eaton, J. and Gersovits, M. (1981), 'Debt with Potential Repudiation', *Review of Economic Studies.*

Eaton, J. and Gersovits, M. (1981b), 'Country Risk: Economic Aspects' in Richard Herring ed., *Managing international risk,* Cambridge University Press, New York, pp.75–108.

Eaton, J. and Gersovits, M. and Stiglitz, J.E. (1986), 'The Pure Theory of Country Risk', *European Economic Review.*

Edwards, S. (1983), 'LDC Foreign Borrowing and Default Risk: an Empirical Investigation, 1976–80'. Working paper no.1172, National Bureau of Economic Research, Cambridge, Mass.

Erbe, R., and Schattner, S. (1980), 'Indicator Systems for the Assessment of The External Debt Situation of Developing Countries', *Intereconomics.*

Export and Import Bank of the U.S. (1976), 'A Survey of Country Evaluation Systems in Use', Washington, D.C.

Fama, E. and Miller, M. (1972), *The Theory of Finance,* New York.

Feder, G. (1978), 'Economic Growth, Foreign Loans, and Debt Service Capacity of Developing Countries', World Bank Staff Working Papers, no.274, Washington, D.C.

Feder, G. (1981), 'Growth and External Borrowing in Trade Gap Economies of Less Developed Countries' *Aussenwirtschaft.*

Feder, G. and Just, R. (1976), 'A Study of Debt Service Capacity Applying Logit Analysis', *Journal of Development Economics.*

Feder, G., Just, R. and Ross, K. (1981), 'Projecting Debt Service Capacity of Developing Countries', *Journal of Financial and Quantitative Analysis.*

Fernandez, R. and Kaaret, D. (1988), 'Bank Size, Reputation and Debt Renegotiation', NBER Working Paper, no.2704, National Bureau of Economic Research, Cambridge, Mass.

Fernandez, R. and Rosenthal, R. (1988), 'Sovereign-Debt Renegotiations: A Strategic Analysis', NBER Working Paper no.2597, National Bureau of Economic Research, Cambridge, Mass.

Fernandez, R. and Glater, J. (1989), 'Why Haven't Debtor Countries Formed a Cartel?', NBER Working Paper, no.2980, National Bureau of Economic Research, Cambridge, Mass.

Frank, C. and Cline, W. (1971), 'Measurement of Debt Servicing Capacity: an Application of Discriminant Analysis', *Journal of International Economics.*

Friedman, I. (1983), The World Debt Dilemma: Managing Country Risk Washington, D.C.: Council for International Banking Studies and Philadelphia: Robert Morris Associates.

Folkerts-Landau, D.F.J. (1985), 'The Changing Role of Bank Lending in Development Finance', *International Monetary Fund Staff Papers,* 32, 317–363.

Gersovitz, M. (1985), 'Banks' International Lending Decisions: What We Know and Implications For Future Research' in Gordon, W.S. and Cuddington, J.T. eds. *International Debt and the Developing Countries,* IBRD, Washington D.C.

Green, H.A. (1971), *Consumer Theory,* Penguin Modern Economic Texts, Cox and Wyman Ltd., London.

Goldberger, A.S. (1964), *Econometric Theory,* John Wiley and Sons, New York.

Goodman, L.S. (1981), 'Bank Lending to Non-OPEC LDC's: Are Risks Diversifiable?', in *Federal Reserve Bank of New York Quarterly Bulletin.*

Goodman, S. (1977), 'How the Big U.S. Banks Really Evaluate Sovereign Risk', in *Euromoney.*

Griffith-Jones, S. ed. (1988), *Managing World Debt,* Harvester Wheatsheaf, New York.

Grinols, E. (1976), 'International Debt Rescheduling and Discrimination Using Financial Variables', U.S. Treasury Department mimeo, Washington, D.C.

Grossman, H. and Van Huyck, J. (1988), 'Sovereign Debt as a Contingent Claim: Excusable Default, Repudiation and Reputation', *American Economic Review.*

Gutentag, J. and Herring, R. (1983), 'Overexposure of International Banks to Country Risk: Diagnosis and Remedies' Testimony before the U.S. Congress, House Committee on Banking, Finance, and Urban Affairs, Subcommittee on International Trade, Investment, and Monetary Policy, 98 Cong., I sess. Washington.

—— (1983), 'The Lender-of-Last-Resort Function in an International Context' *Essays in International Finance,* no.151, Princeton, NJ: International Finance Section, Department of Economics, Princeton University.

Hardy, C.V. (1981), 'Rescheduling Developing-Country Debts', *The Banker,* pp.33–8.

Hardy, C.V. (1982), 'Rescheduling Developing-Country Debts, 1956–1981: lessons and recommendations', Overseas Development Council monograph no.15, Washington, D.C.

Hefferman, S. *et. al.*, (1983), 'Predicting Sovereign Debt Rescheduling', *City University Business School Economic Review,* Autumn.

Hefferman, S. (1985), 'Country Risk Analysis: the Demand and Supply of Sovereign Debt', Journal of International Money and Finance.

Hefferman, S. (1986), *Sovereign Risk Analysis,* Unwin Hyman, London.

Hellwig, M.F. (1977), 'A Model of Borrowing and Lending With Bankruptcy', *Econometrics.*

Institutional Investor (1980), 'The Credit Rating Shake Up', *Institutional Investor,* September.

Jaffee, D. and Modigliani, F. (1969), 'A Theory of Credit Rationing', *American Economic Review.*

Jaffee, D.M. and Modigliani, F. (1969), 'A Theory and Test of Credit Rationing', *American Economic Review.*

Jaffee, D.M. and Russell, T. (1976), 'Imperfect Information, Uncertainty and Credit Rationing', *Quarterly Journal of Economics.*

Kaletsky, A. *The Costs of Default,* New York: Priority Press, 1985.

Keynes, J.M. (1924), 'Foreign Investment and National Advantage', *The Nation and Atheneum.*

Kharas, H. (1981), 'Constrained Optimal Foreign Borrowing by Less Developed Countries', *Mimeo,* Development Policy Staff, World Bank.

Kharas, H. (1984), 'The Long Run Creditworthiness of Developing Countries: Theory and Practice', *Quarterly Journal of Economics.*

Kletzer, K. (1984), 'Asymmetries of Information and LDC Borrowing with Sovereign Risk', *Economic Journal.*

Kletzer, K. (1986), 'External Borrowing by LDC's: A Survey of Theoretical Issues', Yale University Economic Growth Center, Discussion Paper no. 523.

Kreps, D. and Wilson, R. (1982), 'Reputation and Imperfect Information', *Journal of Economic Theory.*

Krueger, A., Harberger, A., Edwards, S. and McKinnon, R. (1990), 'Developing Countries' Debt Problems and Efforts to Policy Reform', *Contemporary Policy Issues.*

Krugman, P. (1985) 'International Debt in an Uncertain World', in Gordon W. Smith and John T. Cuddington,*International Debt and the Developing Countries,* Washington: IBRD.

Krugman, P. (1987), 'Financing vs Forgiving a Debt Overhang: Some Analytical Rates', mimeo, MIT.

Lomax, D. (1983), 'Sovereign Risk Analysis Now', *The Banker.*

Maroni, Y. (1977), 'Approaches for Assessing the Risk Involved in Lending to Developing Countries', Board of Governors of the Federal Reserve System International Finance Discussion Papers, No.112.

Mayo, A.L. and Barret, A.G. (1977), 'An Early-Warning Model for Assessing Developing-Country Risk', in S.H. Goodman (ed.), *Financing and Risk in Developing Countries,* Export-Import Bank, Washington, D.C.

McFadden, D. (1973), 'Conditional Logit Analysis of Qualitative Choice Behaviour', in P. Zarembka, (ed.). *Frontiers in Econometrics,* Academic Press, New York.

McFadden, D. (1976), 'A Comment on Discriminant Analysis 'Versus' Logit Analysis', *Annals of Economic and Social Measurement.*

Nagy, P.J. (1976), 'The Debt Service Ratio: How Useful a Tool', *The Banker.*

Nagy, P.J. (1978), 'Quantifying Country Risk: a System Developed by Economists at the Bank of Montreal', *Columbia Journal of World Business.*

Nagy, P.J. (1979), *Country Risk: How to Assess, Quantify and Monitor It.* Euromoney Publications.

Portes, R. (1987), 'Debt and the Market', CEPR.

Powell, A. (1990), 'The Management of Risk in Developing Country Finance', *Oxford Review of Economic Policy.*

Press, S.J. and Wilson, S. (1978), 'Choosing Between Logistic Regression and Discriminant Analysis', *Journal of the American Statistical Association.*

Sachs, J. (1981),'The Current Account and Macroeconiomic Adjustment in the 1970's, *Brookings Papers on Economic Activity.*

—— (1982), 'LDC Debt: Problems and Prospects', in P. Wachtel (ed.), *Crises in the Economic and Financial Structure,* Lexington Books.

—— (1984), 'Theoretical Issues in International Borrowing', *Princeton Studies in International Finance,* n.54.

—— (1982), 'Stabilization Policies in The World Economy: Scope and Skepticism', National Bureau of Economic Research Working Paper No.862, Cambridge Mass.

—— (1982), 'LDC Debt in the 1980s: Risk & Reforms', National Bureau of Economic Research Working Paper No.861, Cambridge, Mass.

—— (1988), 'The Debt Overhang of Developing Countries' in Macedo and Findlay (ed.) *Debt, Growth and Stabilization: Essays in Memory of Carlos Dias Alejandro,* Oxford, Blackwell.

—— (1989), *Developing Country Debt and the World Economy,* The University of Chicago Press, Chicago.

—— (1990), 'A Strategy for Efficient Debt Reduction', *Journal of Economic Perspectives,* Winter.

Sachs, J. and D. Cohen (1985), 'LDC Borrowing with Default Risk', *Kredit and Kapital,* Special Issue on International Banking.

Sachs, J. and H. Huizinga (1987), 'US Commercial Banks and the Developing-Country Debt Crisis', *Brooking Papers on Economic Activity,* n.2.

Saini, K. and Bates, P. (1978), 'Statistical Techniques for Determining Debt-Servicing Capacity For Developing Countries: Analystical Review of the Literature and Further Empirical Results', Federal Reserve Bank of New York Research Paper no.7818, New York.

Sargen, N. (1977), "Economic Indicators and Country Risk Appraisal', *Federal Reserve Bank of San Francisco Economic Review,* San Francisco, pp.19–35.

Shapiro, A.C. (1982), 'Risk in International Banking', *Journal of Financial and Quantitative Analysis.*

Simonsen, M.H. (1985), 'The Developing-Country Debt Problem' in Gordon, W.S. and Cuddington, J.T. eds., *International Debt and The Developing Countries,* IBRD, Washington D.C., pp.101–126.

Smith, G.W. (1975), "Quantitive Approaches to Forecasting Debt Service Problems', *Mimeo,* Washington, DC.

Smith, G.W (1977), 'The External Debt Prospects of The Non-Oil Exporting Developing Countries: an Econometric Analysis', Overseas Development Council NIEO Series, Monograph no.10,Washington, DC.

Solomon, R. (1977), 'A Perspective on The Debt of Developing Countries', *Brookings Papers on Economic Activity,* no.2.

Solomon, R. (1981), 'The Debt of Developing Countries: Another Look', *Brookings Papers on Economic Activity,* no.2.

Stiglitz, J. and Weiss, A. (1981), 'Credit Rationing in Markets with Imperfect Information: I', *American Economic Review.*

Walter, I. (1981), 'Country Risk, Portfolio Decisions and Regulation in International Bank Lending', *Journal of Banking and Finance.*

Index